Real Housewives of Diplomacy:
A Psychological Study

Nicole Nasr

Real Housewives of Diplomacy: A Psychological Study

Nicole Nasr

St. James's Studies in World Affairs
Academica Press
Washington – London

Library of Congress Cataloging-in-Publication Data

Names: Nasr, Nicole, author.
Title: Real housewives of diplomacy : a psychological study / Nicole Nasr.
Other titles: Lived experience of wives of diplomats
Description: Washington : Academica Press, 2019. | Series: St. James's studies in world affairs | Revision of author's thesis (doctoral)--City University (London, England), 2018 titled The lived experience of wives of diplomats : an interpretative phenomenological analysis. | Summary: "This is a psychological study of wives of diplomats"-- Provided by publisher.
Identifiers: LCCN 2019012301 | ISBN 9781680534894 (hardcover) | ISBN 9781680531527 (paperback)
Subjects: LCSH: Diplomats' spouses--Psychology. | Diplomats--Family relationships. | Women--Identity--Case studies. | Marriage--Psychological aspects.
Classification: LCC JZ1418 .N37 2019 | DDC 327.2086/55--dc23
LC record available at https://lccn.loc.gov/2019012301

Contents

List of Tables and Figures

Acknowledgements

I would first like to acknowledge the courage of the eight Wives of Diplomats ("WODs") who participated in this study. I thank you for trusting me with your stories and allowing me to become a part of them.

To my supervisor, Dr. George Berguno, your support, dedication, and faith in my topic have meant a lot to me. You have affected my stance on social justice by opening my eyes and allowing me to look beneath the surface, and for that I am very grateful.

I would like to also thank from the bottom of my heart my parents, William and Lina, for their financial and emotional support throughout this journey. You have made countless sacrifices for me, and I truly hope to always make you proud. To William and Cynthia, you are the best siblings one could ask for and your support has meant the world to me. I love you more than you will ever know!

To my friends in Beirut, London, Washington, and Montreal, you have made this journey manageable. From talking about the thesis on which this book is based to knowing when I needed to detach, your presence in my life is one that I cherish deeply. I would like to thank especially my best friend Cindy Menassa, whose weekly calls this last year have allowed me to breath at times when I felt suffocated. Thank you, thank you, thank you!

I would like to also thank Myriam Osorio Azzi for inspiring me with this topic. Your courage for opening up to me about diplomatic life was my first step towards this book. I will be eternally grateful for your constant efforts and encouragements.

Most importantly, I would like to acknowledge and thank the man of my dreams, Alex Azzi. You have been part of this journey since the day I decided to apply to my doctoral program, and none of this would have been possible without your patience, support, and reassurance. You are my backbone. I love you!

Finally, it is with tears of sadness and joy that I would like to dedicate this book to my uncle Richard, who has unfortunately left us too early. Ever since I can remember, he dedicated time to knowing and understanding me, and as a result encouraged me to enter the field of psychology. I thank him for making me the woman I am today and promise to devote both time and effort in guiding his two precious boys the same way he guided me. I miss him every day.

Preface

This book includes three sections: a research study, an analytical discussion, and a clinical case study. Their common theme is dependency and female empowerment as seen in diplomatic wives' identities in relation to their husbands.

The first section is an empirical study exploring the experience of being a "Wife of a Diplomat" (WOD) across diplomatic assignments. For several decades, women have separated from the traditional norm, as society increasingly expects them to make independent decisions and create their own personal paths and careers. One subgroup that has yet to experience this shift is spouses of diplomats. Accompanying a spouse in diplomatic mobility has long been associated with the image of a dependent and nonworking wife (Fechter, 2010) whose domestic work has been incorporated into the corporate ideologies (Callan & Ardener, 1984). As a result, many WODs have been unable to experience women's empowerment in the traditionally patriarchal world of diplomacy. This phenomenon has been poorly explored, leaving many WODs feeling unheard, undervalued, and unaccounted for (Hendry, 1998). This book seeks not only to fill the gap, but to also raise awareness in the research community and shed light on a hidden minority that has been overlooked. I interviewed eight participants about their experiences as WODs and analyzed data using Interpretive Phenomenological Analysis, or "IPA" (Smith, 2017). Emergent themes reflected on the ways in which WODs struggled to make sense of their presence during diplomatic postings. The study pays careful attention to factors that supported and impeded WODs' senses of self and explores the different ways they were able to manage these difficulties.

While my aim was to understand these women's subjective experiences and allow them to share their stories by giving them a voice, my initial interest stemmed from a personal difficulty witnessing injustice and unfairness. Indeed, shortly before commencing my DPsych training in counseling psychology in London, I lived and studied in Beirut, Lebanon, where I met my fiancé. As he is the son of a diplomat, I took great interest in his mother's life, thinking that she was very lucky to have lived such a glamorous life. She quickly corrected me by allowing me to see the reality behind the closed doors of the diplomatic world. She shared with me many stories of other WODs, which revealed injustice and unfairness that I did not understand at the time. I soon realized that feminist values triggered this reaction, helping me see that many WODs suffered in silence and rarely sought help. Wanted to explore this further, I engaged in many conversations with friends of my fiancé's family and realized that many shared common experiences.

The second section of this book is an empirical study that draws on the qualitative research presented above. This section focuses on diplomatic marriages, which could allow WODs to lose their senses of self and make sense of who they became throughout their diplomatic journeys. This article considers ways in which WODs' experiences seemed to have been shaped by the diplomatic world's patriarchal norms. Implications for psychological practitioners are also discussed in terms of their clinical work. Finally, this section suggests the responsibility of psychologists to advocate for social justice and become part of a community psychology.

The last section is a case study representing my therapeutic work with one client who was in the process of divorcing her husband. It was taken from my final year placement and reflected my clinical practice from a person-centered approach. This approach was best suited to show the client that her relationship does not have to be dominated by her husband's agenda, and that the locus of control can and should be within her (Mearns & Cooper, 2005; Rogers, 1957). I have chosen to present this client as she both evoked in me similar feelings of unfairness when I first heard stories of WODs and influenced my professional and personal development as a woman.

One of the threads that unites the sections discussed above is the issue of dependency. This book is at heart the story of women who have to some extent experienced a sense of dependency on their spouses, which has affected their identities and senses of self. It feels only natural to acknowledge the element of empowerment throughout their processes of sense-making. Indeed, throughout their diplomatic journey, WODs have enhanced their senses of empowerment by finding ways of managing, understanding, and shifting their perceptions. As all embarked on their husband's journey, they aimed for self-development separate from their husbands' lives and careers. Similarly, the work done with my client, presented at the end, was mainly based on empowerment, helping her develop a strong, stable, and independent identity that was not influenced by her husband's views and beliefs.

As I approached the end of my training, I realized how this study has influenced my views of relationships and marriage. The experience of engaging it has compelled me to reflect on the kind of wife I want to be for my future husband, while reminding me of the importance of staying congruent within myself. I have also found myself affirming the importance of one's professional identity and discussing with my fiancé the extent to which I would be willing to shift from it. Finally, this book has empowered me to take control over the fluidity of my identity, and to always empathize and support others who cannot.

Chapter 1- Critical Literature Review

1.1 Diplomacy[1] in its Dimensions

1.1.1 Historical Background on Diplomacy

Diplomacy is one of the oldest forms of expatriate assignment. Although Greek, Roman, and Byzantine models of diplomacy dominated for a long period, modern diplomacy can be traced to the states of Northern Italy in the Middle Ages, with the first embassies, in the modern sense, founded in the thirteenth century by the Duchy of Milan and emulated by other states. They created many of the traditions of modern diplomacy, such as the presentation of an ambassador's credentials to the host country's head of state.

At the time, and until quite recently in at least the European experience, ambassadors were mainly noblemen whose status differed with the prestige of the country to which they were posted. Important defining standards emerged for ambassadors, requiring them to have large residences, host lavish parties, and play important roles in the court life of their host country. Although many noblemen had few skills in foreign relations, they were supported by a large staff with expertise in the host country and formal protocol. In the centuries that followed, permanent

---

[1] Of course, it should be noted that individual countries have different work specifications for their diplomats, and different rights for their spouses. While one responsibility/right may be required/available by one country, another may find it irrelevant.

foreign offices were founded in many European countries in order to coordinate staff members and embassies.

Until the 1980s, diplomats were almost always chosen for their professional competencies and (male) gender, but were also favored for their marital status. In France, for example, it was inconceivable for diplomats to hold diplomatic postings without the presence of a spouse, which was considered prerequisite (De Singly & Chaland, 2002). Diplomatic candidates were thus evaluated on the basis of gender and marital status as well as professional competency, leading them to label their spouses' presence as crucial to their postings, and even referring to her as an auxiliary to the diplomat (De Singly & Chaland, 2002).

1.1.2 Diplomatic Roles and Responsibilities

Diplomats represent their countries abroad while involved in the act of diplomacy. This act is defined as the art and practice of conducting negotiations between nations without arousing hostility. Diplomatic missions are characterized by the basic functions they are intended to provide, such as protecting the interests of the home country and its citizens in the host country. Other functions include negotiating with the host government; monitoring and reporting on conditions and developments in the commercial, economic, cultural, and scientific life of the host country; and issuing passports, travel documents, and visas (Hockings, 2006).

One important diplomatic duty is the need to build relationships and improve contact with the host country. In this role, diplomats offer guidance to their host countries on topics that affect the well-being of the people and governments of both host and home countries. Diplomats usually accomplish these tasks by connecting with leaders and decisionmakers in both governments, and local community members and leaders (Hockings, 2006).

Some countries' diplomats take on different roles within their respective foreign services, and diplomats can perform multiple duties on behalf of their home countries while serving abroad. The United States Foreign Service, for example, separates its officers into five distinct career subjects, referred to as "cones," and diplomats choose their cone at the beginning of their careers (Hockings, 2006). These can be consular, political, economic, managerial, or in the realm of public diplomacy (Hockings, 2006). Each "cone" represents a different set of responsibilities and burdens carried by the diplomat and his team. As a result, many spouses will find themselves more or less involved in official representation depending on the chosen cone.

Readers may ask what relevance the history and the roles of diplomats have to the research question my project seeks to answer. I feel it is important to consider how diplomats, their spouses, and others view the world of diplomacy and understand its origins, as they may have been influenced by it. It is diplomats' predecessors who lived through this time and formed the image of what is now known as diplomatic postings and diplomacy. The effect this has had on my participants' experiences will be explored further in subsequent chapters.

1.2 Theories of Identity

In the past few decades, the subject of identity has been widely researched and theorized in psychology (Breakwell, 1986; Côté, 2006) as a result of the concern with the self. The notion of identity appears to have been used interchangeably with other closely related concepts, such as self, self-identity, and self-concept, to name only a few. Vignoles,

Schwartz, and Luyckx (2011) argue that "identity" is a complex and sometimes even "obscure" term that can mean different things depending on researchers' philosophical and theoretical models. Assuming that each cultural era influenced our understanding of the self and identity, Logan (1987) emphasized that this current concern is a result of our existentialist postmodern era, and that it allowed people to gain a psychological perspective and develop a stronger sense of self (Vignoles, et al., 2011).

In this project, I consider the definition of identity as "who you act as being" in relation to others, and "who you think you are" as a member of a specific group and as an individual (Vignoles et al., 2011, p. 2). I also adopt a "light" social constructionist epistemology, which will be discussed further in the next chapter. I took this epistemological position because social context is a significant element in the construction of the self (Gergen, 1985). Hence, theories of identity presented in this research look through the framework of subjective experience, and I will review theoretical perspectives within a personal and social context. These will be discussed in relation to frequent relocations and the state of being an accompanying spouse, while focusing on their effect on self-esteem and self-concept.

1.2.1 Interactionism and Identity

Howard (2000) offered a contextual definition of identity that stems from symbolic-interactionism. She explained that the basic premise of symbolic interaction is that people attach symbolic meaning to behaviors, other people, objects, and themselves (Howard, 2000). These meanings are developed and transmitted through interactions and can vary in their emphasis. As a result, Howard (2000) used the concept of identity to locate an individual within a "social space by virtue of the relationships that these identities [implied], and [were], themselves, symbols whose meanings [varied] across actors and situations" (Howard, 2000, p. 371). In other words, people behave toward objects on the grounds of the meanings these objects have for them and not on the basis of their concrete properties.

The interactionist approach to identity focuses on (1) the structure of identity and (2) the interactions and processes through which it is constructed. Howard's (2000) structural approach relies mainly on the concept of role identities and on the characters a person develops as the occupant of a specific social position, explicitly linking social structures to the person. Hence, self-identity is an ensemble of role-identities that are hierarchically organized according to the importance they have in a person's life and the degree to which one is committed to them (Howard, 2000). This degree of commitment "depends on the extent to which these identities are premised on our ties to particular other people" (Howard, 2000, p. 371). The second approach focuses on the processes of identity construction and negotiation. Negotiations about who a person is are fundamental to the development of mutual definitions of situations as they entail impression management and self-presentation (Goffman, 1959; Howard, 2000; McCall & Simmons, 1978). As a result, for Howard (2000) identities are strategic social constructions created through interactions, with material and social consequences.

1.2.2 Social Identity Theory

Thinking about identity as group memberships, Tajfel and Turner (1986) developed Social Identity Theory (SIT), which focuses on the extent to which individuals think and identify themselves in terms of groups. The centrality of SIT is characterized by individuals defining their identities by following two dimensions: The personal - the idiosyncratic elements that differentiate an individual from others; and the social - defined by a sense of belonging in various social groups. Although Tajfel and Turner (1986) view identities lying at different ends of the spectrum, Deaux (1993) argues for an interplay between both dimensions, suggesting that they cannot easily be separable. Deaux (1993) adds that people's identities are anchored within their surrounding social environments, as they focus on wider social groups and context. She adds that through this social perspective, identity cannot be viewed as a static and rigid structure, but instead as a combination of convoluted processes. These processes guide individuals in their social worlds, suggesting that identities are subject to change and can be flexible and tailored to specific situations (Bausinger, 1999; Breakwell, 1983; Deaux, 1993).

Others have also stressed the importance of the social dimension as part of our identity (Brewer & Gardner, 1996; Goffman, 1959), resulting from a natural need to belong that affects our inner subjective self-representation. However, some, such as Goffman (1959), express extreme views that the self is strictly a social self, suggesting a narrowed vision of the human world, namely one that is rule-governed, ritualized, and scripted (Jenkins, 2008).

1.2.3 Reflexivity and Identity

The sociologist Anthony Giddens (1991) stressed that self-identity lies within specific temporal and cultural contexts. He considers the role of awareness and reflexivity in an attempt to understand one's identity in terms of his or her biography (Giddens, 1991). These "reflexive projects" require individuals to work, reflect, and review their personal narratives in order to gain meaning. He continues to argue that a stable sense of identity can only be maintained when individuals create an ongoing, coherent narrative of their selves (Giddens, 1991).

Additionally, self-identity in the late modern era seems to differ from earlier traditional societies in that contemporary societies have evolved threats to identities. Giddens (1991) described these threats as "situations where individuals' sense of continuity and security [are] challenged due to increase fragmentation and uncertainty" (p. 243). Giddens (1991) has been criticized, however, for holding dualistic views of body and mind by failing to account for experiences of embodiment, despite his acknowledgment of the role of the body as a reflexive project (Shilling & Mellor, 1996). Other researchers remind us that identity should be perceived as a subjective psychological experience, given that both identity management and change occur within a constant process of interaction (Vignoles, Regalia, Manzi, Golledge & Scabini, 2006). Taking place in a particular cultural context, these interactions occur between individuals' social worlds and their active reflexivity. Additionally, Linstead and Thomas (2002) refer to identity as a "project, not an achievement," suggesting that it is a constant developing concept, persistently influenced by one's active reflections.

1.2.4 Identity Process Theory

Some might critique these theories as one-sided, not taking into consideration one's personal striving for continuity and the impact that biography has in forming identity. As Glynis Breakwell (1986) saw a need to focus on both the social and psychological processes that form identities, she developed Identity Process Theory (IPT) in order to address these issues. Having worked with Henri Tajfel on SIT (Tajfel, 1978),

Breakwell paid great attention to assimilating both social and personal identities, arguing that both are part of the individual's biography.

Breakwell (2010) suggested that the fundamental element to understanding identity was to examine an individual's response when his or her identity is threatened. IPT is concerned with the holistic examination of an individual's identity as a whole and proposes elements that result dynamically from aspects of individual experiences, such as group memberships, interpersonal relationships, social representations, personal experiences, and more. At the core of IPT is the affirmation that individuals seek to construct and maintain certain identities by engaging in constant negotiation between individuals and their surroundings. Furthermore, individuals are seen to have control over the construction of their identity, although Jaspal (2011) argues that this degree of agency may be constrained by the overriding social representations of a particular social context. I have chosen to include IPT because it focuses on the social and psychological processes that form an individual's identity, rather than solely looking at identity as evolving from evaluations of social processes.

In IPT, identity is assumed to be regulated by the processes of accommodation/assimilation and evaluation, which are thought to be universal psychological processes. Assimilation and accommodation are two components of the same process: respectively, one refers to the inclusion of new components into an identity structure, and the other refers to the adjustment that happens in the existing structure so space can be made for new elements. Evaluation, on the other hand, is the process by which an individual gives value and meaning to the contents of identity.

Over time, both processes interact to determine the changing value and content of one's identity. Although she recognized that historical and cultural specifics can have an impact, Breakwell (2010) offered four discernible principles that guide these processes: Continuity of the self through time, distinctiveness as a positive sense of uniqueness, self-esteem, and self-efficacy. Self-esteem is defined as varying on the extent of effective actions and social approval of others (Breakwell & Lyons, 1996). As a result of the considerable amount of debate about these principles, Jaspal (2011) suggested that three more principles, namely meaning, belonging, and psychological coherence between identities, should be added to Breakwell's.

These dynamic processes raise great challenges in terms of management of multiple conflicting social groups and situations involving threats to one's identity. In other words, as individuals move within the social structure, threats to identity can be experienced when changes conflict with the principles that guide them. Breakwell (1986) termed this problem "Identity Threat" and defined it as "a threat to identity [that] occurs when the process of identity, assimilation-accommodation and evaluation are, for some reason, unable to comply with the principles of continuity, distinctiveness and self-esteem, which habitually guide their operation" (p. 47), taking the form of an attack.

Breakwell (1986) explained that individuals may use a range of coping strategies, categorized as deflecting or accepting. Strategies of deflection include avoidance and/or denial of the existent threat and negativity toward or confrontation of the source. Acceptance strategies, on the other hand, include a reevaluation of principles and/or a fundamental identity change as a result of the threats.

1.2.5 Mead's (1934) Theory of Self

The philosopher G.H. Mead (1934) explained in his book *Mind, Self and Society* that the self is a social emergent and the individual self is a product of social interaction rather than biological or logical conditions. Indeed, he argued that the self is a developmental process and is not there at birth: It arises in the process of activities and social experiences, and develops within the individual as a result of his relations within himself and others (Mead, 1934). As Mead (1934) distinguished the "self" from the "body," he asked, "How can an individual get outside himself, experientially, in such a way as to become an object to himself?" (p. 221). He attempted to answer this question by explaining that the "self" can only be understood in terms of social interaction with others. Indeed, individuals experience themselves indirectly from the standpoints of other individuals of the same social group, or from generalized standpoints of social group to which they belong. As such, individuals can "enter as objects [to themselves] only on the basis" of these interactions (Mead, 1934, p. 225), and engage in self-consciousness. Mead (1934) defined self-consciousness as a process by which individuals take the attitude of others towards themselves and attempt to view themselves from the standpoint of others. He develops his account of the self's social emergence further by elucidating three forms of intersubjective activity: language, play, and game. These methods of symbolic interaction, which include words, gestures, and roles, are the founding paradigms of his theory of socialization and form the basic "social processes that render the reflexive objectification of the self possible" (Madzia, 2013, p. 208).

Although the self is a product of socio-symbolic interactions, it is not a passive echoing of the other's views and standpoints. Instead, individuals' responses to their social world are active, given that individuals consciously decide how they will react to others' attitudes. Mead (1934) proposed two poles of the self that determine these reactions: 1) the pole that reflects the attitude of the other and 2) the pole that responds to the attitude of the other. This separation resulted in the distinguishing of the "me" from the "I." Mead (1934) defined the "I" as the "response of the organism to the attitudes of the others; and the "me" [as] "the organized set of attitudes of others which one assumes" (p. 175). It appears that a dialectical relationship exists between the individual and society, which influences the intrapsychic levels of this polarity. Indeed, the "me" is the internalization of roles, which derive from the socio-symbolic processes, and the "I" is the creative response to the socio-symbolized structure of the "me." However, although it could be tempting to view both as separate entities of the self, it is more accurate to see them as a dynamic relationship that forms the self (Margolis & Catudal, 2001).

1.2.6 Social Self-Identity and Social Media

The self can be classified into two categories: 1) an individual self-identity and 2) a social self-identity (Carter & Grover, 2015). The first emerges from one's autonomy and can distinguish itself from others, while the second "refers to the categorizations of the self that reflect assimilation to more inclusive social units" (Carter & Grover, 2015, p. 940). In recent years, social self-identity has become more significant as different social environments surround individuals, leading them to define themselves through others. More than ever before, individuals are now more pre-occupied by how others perceive them, thus affecting the way they see and experience themselves (Pan, Lu, Wang & Chau, 2017). A current important vehicle for self-presentation has been the use of social media platforms (Chen, Lu, Chau & Gupta, 2014).

In contrast to other traditional modes of expression, social media is far more complex as it gives a more salient role to the self-presentation process and manipulates the image received by the audience (DeVito, Brinholtz & Hancock, 2017). However, studies have linked social media use with certain negative effects on well-being, affecting the quality of life of many individuals (Appel, Gerlach & Crusius, 2016; Meier, Reinecke & Meltzer, 2916). An important study conducted by Woods and Scott (2016) showed that social media use was related to poorer sleep quality, lower self-esteem, and higher levels of depression and anxiety. They justified these results by examining the amount of time adolescents spent on social media and the emotional investment they had in social media platforms (Woods & Scott, 2016).

Although much social media research has focused on teenagers, Vogel, Rose, Roberts, and Eckles (2014) have studied the effect of social media on adults and found similar results. They explained that social media offered abundant opportunities for upward social comparison, leading to changes in individuals' self-evaluation processes (Vogel, et al., 2014). Indeed, they explained that although upward social comparison can be beneficial, as it inspires individuals to become more like their comparison targets (Lockwood & Kunda, 1997), when linked to social media, it engendered feelings of inadequacy, negative affect, unpopularity, and poorer self-evaluation (Kim & Lee, 2011; Vitak & Ellison, 2013). A more recent study showed how one's fears of missing out ("FOMO") and being disconnected from others have contributed to poorer mental health among adults (Dhir, Yossatorn, Kaur & Chen, 2018). Indeed, several studies have showed that social media users with these particular fears are more likely to suffer from negative emotions, depression, poor sleep, compulsive social media use (Baker et al., 2016), low life satisfaction, low personal interconnection, emotional tension, and problems with emotional control (Elhai, et al., 2016; Wolniewicz et al., 2018). Many social media scholars have explained that such reactions to high social media use often result from an incoherent sense of self (Aalbers et al., 2018; Vogel et al., 2014). Indeed, individuals who experience an unstable sense of self are more likely to be affected by social media than individuals who experience stronger self-identity (Aalbers et al., 2018).

1.2.7 Conclusion on the Theories of Identity

Theories of identity have left a gap for further exploration into the subjective experiences of identity and threats to it. Further research may help us understand how identity threats are experienced and understood when a lack of agency, frequent relocation, and loss of professional identity can occur. Due to the great impact of social media on individuals who experience unstable senses of self, it would be interesting to see if, and how, social media has affected WODs. Although some qualitative studies have attempted to explore frequent relocations and their link to being an accompanying spouse (e.g. Arieli, 2007; Davoine, Ravasi, Salamin & Cudre-Mauroux, 2012; De Singly & Challand, 2002), there has been little attention to studying these different experiences from a phenomenological standpoint.

1.3 Diplomacy and its Impacts

1.3.1 Frequent Relocation and the Psychological Implications

A common understanding of mobility is the movement of the body between different locations in geographical space. This experience, mainly characterized by the concept of change, has been found to have far-reaching implications for the psychological well-being of people, as it can threaten self-concept (Davis, 2011). Identity threats can be experienced when conflicts between the identity components and values of individuals clash, leading to significant psychological effects on the individual's well-being. Vignoles et al. (2006) argued that when individuals' self-esteem is threatened, psychological well-being is affected, leading them to attempt to minimize the damages or reevaluate certain components of their identities (Sedikides & Gregg, 2003). As geographic space and mobility play an important role in identity, researchers have concluded that it has become a potential identity threat to many who are subject to these moves (Easthope, 2009; Hardwick, 2003; McHugh, 2000; Silvey & Lawson, 1999). Jones (1997) suggested that as a result of the changes and transitions, these threats can have a potential effect on an individual's identity processes, such as a relative shift in the prominence of different identity dimensions. Hence, many identity dimensions such as professional, national, and ethnic components may require reevaluation (Easthope, 2009; Jones, 1997).

With regard to diplomatic mobility, Nicholson's (1984) theory of work role transitions shows that diplomats tend to follow the replication adjustment strategy when experiencing change as they make some adjustments to their identities in order to fit into their roles (De Singly &

Chaland, 2002). Although they experience different countries at each assignment, their overall social role stays the same, meaning that they experience fewer effects on their self-identity (De Singly & Challand, 2002). In contrast, a WOD's identity may be deeply affected by frequent relocations as she leaves behind formed social identities, such as a professional one, in order to take on a new identity as a WOD (Arieli, 2007; Collins & Bertone, 2017; Davoine et al., 2012; De Singly & Challand, 2002).

Frequent mobility may pose a threat to identity by violating one or more of the guiding principles of identity, as proposed by IPT (Breakwell, 1986). Diplomatic assignments take place in different social, national, and developmental domains, hence influencing diplomatic families' inner selves, social relations, and life choices (e.g. leaving a career, choosing a university major), all of which have implications for the construction of a WOD's separate identity. These threats can result from families' transitions and their experience of precarity, characterized by the instability of occupational identities and the unpredictability of the next diplomatic assignment (Cangià, 2018).

Diplomatic and consular professionals are considered to be higher civil servants, like the French prefects of De Singly and Chaland's (2002) study, who highlighted many common characteristics with international executives, such as high-level qualifications and high professional mobility with different levels of responsibilities. The regular international assignment rhythm is between two to four years in international postings, with optional periods of two years in the home country between each posting (Davoine et al., 2012). Diplomatic assignments are initiated by a government's ministry of foreign affairs, which appoints diplomats to temporary missions in variable locations, making their assignments usually unpredictable in both timing and location.

The study of daily experiences raises important questions about the meaning and experience of global mobility, and the movement of family members who have long been viewed as "privileged" travelers (Beaverstock, 2002; Cranston, 2016; Meier, 2014; Smith & Favell, 2006). Although diplomatic mobility represents an important component of frequent migration flows, it is an inherently and unavoidably stressful way of life (Ravasi, Salamin & Davoine, 2013).

International relocation stress has been defined by Wilkinson and Singh (2010) as "a psychological state that develops when an individual faces a situation that taxes or exceeds internal or external resources available to deal with that situation" (p. 169). Wilkinson and Singh (2010) referred to three major components of stress: lack of control over situations, uncertainty concerning outcomes, and ambiguity concerning expectations. Hence, "by their very nature, overseas assignments are characterized by uncertainty, lack of control and ambiguity" (Wilkinson & Singh, 2010, p. 169). When considering the Holmes and Rahe (1967) stress scale, at least half of the forty most stressful life events can be directly or indirectly related to the diplomatic families' uprooting from their home country and engaging in diplomatic mobility. These life events include a change in financial status (15th on the scale); change or new line of work (17th on the scale); spouse starting or stopping a job (25th on the scale); and changes in residence (31st on the scale), school (32nd on the scale), and social activities (34th on the scale).

Beyond the stress of practical mobility and unexpected life events that can take place during an international assignment -- such as bereavement, sickness, fears of kidnapping, and/or host country insecurity (e.g. civil wars) -- diplomats and their families are exposed to higher levels of daily stress compared to non-diplomatic families (Cangià & Zittoun, 2018). They also need to become accustomed to stressors related to cultural, social, legal, religious, political, and environmental adaptation (Niekrenz, Witte & Albrecht, 2016). The uncertainty, lack of control, and ambiguity that characterize diplomatic assignments represent a certain level of stress that can easily shape the quality of life of family members. For example, some studies show that marriage can serve as a shield against everyday stress, including hardships, and can diminish the threat of external events (Pearlin & Johnson, 1977; Sweatman, 1999). However, when a couple experiences too much stress, there can be psychological and/or psycho-physiological consequences (e.g. illness, substance abuse) that can negatively affect the quality of the marriage (McNulty, 2012; Wilkinson & Singh, 2010).

In an important study, McNulty (2012) found that at least six percent of accompanying spouses indicated that they were considering divorce or marital separation as a result of stress-relocation. In comparison, 99 percent of expatriate couples rated a stable and strong marriage as the most important adjustment element when experiencing international assignments. Hyslop (2012) found that 445 expatriate couples living in the United Arab Emirates, for example, ended their marriages in 2011, a 30 percent increase over the 2009 figure. Lazarova, McNulty, and Semeniuk (2015) found that 92 percent of the 650 expatriate families they studied believed that relocation-related marital tension can affect family dynamics, suggesting that more research is needed to explore the unique needs of expatriate families with single, separated, or divorced parents.

1.3.2 The Professional Identity of Wives of Diplomats

One strand that emerges in relevant studies is the link between diplomatic assignments and the issue of spousal identity. Diplomatic mobility can be a profound experience significantly influencing many different aspects of the self, often requiring continuous reevaluation of various identity components and roles (Arieli, 2007; Davoine et al., 2013; De Singly & Chaland, 2002; Dovidio & Esses, 2001). The mobility of diplomats can have an impact on family arrangements and on the spouse's plans and working life, which may involve experiencing breaks in their professional careers and/or various challenges with regards to relocation (Cangià, 2018).

The rise of couples with dual careers and greater awareness of professional identities have recently become important issues, as WODs are becoming more concerned about having professional identities independent of their partners' (Andreason, 2008; Simosi, Rousseau, & Daskalaki, 2015). Many countries have traditionally banned spouses of diplomats from working while on diplomatic postings, due to possible conflicts of interests and a lack of work authorizations. Although some nations (e.g. Sweden) have begun forging bilateral pacts with other countries allowing diplomatic spouses to seek outside employment, the majority of countries still prohibit it. Even when there are such bilateral agreements between countries, however, a WOD's career may be limited due to frequent moves and unstable experiences (Finch, 2012; Pahl & Pahl, 1971).

Accompanying a spouse has long been associated with the image of a dependent and nonworking wife (Fechter, 2010) whose domestic work has been incorporated into the corporate ideologies (Callan & Ardener, 1984). Schaller (1995) found that a decline in personal career among Swiss WODs was higher than expected, with only 16 percent of spouses of diplomats who worked prior to their first posting returning to work and pursuing their chosen professions. Concerns over career prospects also emerged in a study conducted by the Austrian researcher Wille-Romer (1992), who found that 75 percent of participants who had completed some form of professional training were not practicing their professions due to diplomatic assignments.

Given WODs' decline in professional identity, many have experienced a shift in their efforts in their careers to their husbands' careers (Arieli, 2007). These shifts are especially acute for WODs whose husbands' careers entail expectations on them to perform tasks and/or fill roles that serve the diplomatic assignment. Feminist sociologist Papanek (1973), who wrote about American middle-class women married to professionals, termed this concept a "two-person single career." She suggested that this term served as a mechanism of social control that kept wives "in their place" by channeling their personal career aspirations into supporting their husbands' careers, resulting in a psychological cost for women (Papanek, 1973). Papanek described this cost as a destruction of women's self-esteem, as they were expected to conduct tasks they were reluctant to do, while their time and efforts went undervalued. Despite the decades that have passed since her work, similar phenomena have been found in studies of wives of professional baseball players (Ortiz, 1997), clergymen (Frame & Shehan, 1994), business executives (Hochschild,

2003), French government prefects (De Singly & Challand, 2002), and college and university presidents (Reid, Cole & Kern, 2011).

For women, losing one's professional identity can be seen as a central component in their experiences of becoming an accompanying wife. Kanji and Cahusac (2015) have found that the transition from professional to stay-at-home wife and mother was found to be a continuous struggle in which WODs tried to reconcile their professional, spousal, and maternal identities before and after exiting the workplace, illustrating how identity change is a crucial and integral part in workplace exit. Their findings also implied that women pay a high cost from losing their professional identities (Kanji & Cahusac, 2015), while trying to cope with the loss and the disjuncture of exiting the professional world (Howard, 2000). Their subsequent ability to reach the classic action of sense-making enabled these women to reconcile themselves to their loss and perceive their exit as a personal choice. Although Kanji and Cahusac's study is a valuable contribution to understanding the sense-making of identity loss, it does not address the spouse's decision to leave professional life, and the potential effect this might have on the participant's sense-making.

In the case of diplomacy, this process essentially means accompanying the husband to a host country and entering a social structure that is more patriarchal than the one the wives might have experienced in their home countries, especially as professionals. The fact of leaving the workplace makes these wives, some for the first time, financially and socially dependent on their husbands (Arieli, 2007; De Singly & Challand, 2002). Kinsley (1977) highlighted this concept by offering a representation of what economic marital dependency is, suggesting that "at the core of a wife's dependence on her husband is her inferior earning power. As long as she is not able to get a job with pay and prestige at least equivalent to that of her husband, she must rely upon him to maintain her standard of living and social status" (p. 80).

As a result of the lower social status and levels of power, accompanying wives are more likely to have chronic strain and a lower sense of mastery (Nolen-Hoeksema & Davis, 1999). Given their lack of financial contribution, WODs are chiefly responsible for childcare and childrearing, and will tend to subordinate their own needs in order to maintain their relationships and reduce the risks of dissolution (Valor-Segura, Exposito, Moya & Kluwer, 2014). Ultimately, this "silencing of the self" leaves wives feeling "unheard, undervalued and under-appreciated" in their marriages (McBridge & Bagby, 2006, p. 187).

In his *Social Rank Theory*, Paul Gilbert (2000) examined this phenomenon closely by studying subordinate hierarchies. He suggested that threats to identity can be triggered by loss of approval and acceptance by others, and eventually translate into submissive strategies such as shyness, shame, and depression (Berger, Keshet & Gilboa-Schechtman, 2017; Gilbert, 2000). Indeed, Gilbert (2000) explained how humans are concerned with others' levels of approval and value of their personal traits, and tended to internalize these concerns by perceiving themselves in low rank self-relevant domains. He added that this perception made humans feel inferior as they did not feel valued, esteemed, chosen, desired, wanted, and accepted, all part of the concept of involuntary subordinate self-perception (Gilbert, 1992). In relation to WODs, losing one's professional identity can trigger thoughts of "seeing oneself as undesirably inferior to others, less attractive and an outsider, and thus not able to garner the interests and approval of others" (Gilbert, 2000, p. 175). It feels important to note that the unwanted and involuntary nature of this novel social position is an important aspect of the way in which WODs perceive and react to their social ranking. Indeed, this involuntary subordination has been found to affect people's emotional well-being, often effecting the presence and severity of depression, social anxiety, and a poor sense of self (Gilboa-Schechtman, Friedman, Helpman & Kananov, 2013).

1.3.3 Wives of Diplomats in Diplomatic Assignments

Many women have accepted or adopted, to a certain extent, the role of spouse for at least some part of their adult lives. In traditional Western culture (and some current Asian cultures), the role of the "wife" has been defined as caretaker and homemaker of the household and family, while husbands were considered breadwinners and often detached from household affairs. As a result, it is fair to say that many WODs have been expected to accompany their husbands, and support them through diplomatic assignments, even if these expectations are both unofficial and uncompensated.

Among the challenges WODs face is sustaining a sense of self while at the same time performing a traditional female role in a society that increasingly expects of women to make independent decisions and create their own personal paths and careers. In a marriage where the diplomat enjoys a prestigious and well-defined sense of self through his role and professional identity, his spouse may still be expected to play a range of traditional roles. Along with social shifts that have occurred over the past 50 years, various researchers have studied factors affecting marriages, women's employment, and dual careers (e.g. Haring, Hewitt & Flett, 2003; Zuo & Shengming, 2000).

The complexity and difficulty of describing roles and relationships within a marriage has led us to think that married partners are rarely equal in terms of responsibilities, power and status (Dryden, 1999). These inequalities result from the construction of role, and are based on the social norms of gender and related expectations. For women, these norms effected their independent identities as many internalized the notion of limited agency and the importance of self-sacrifice (Beers, 1992; Dressel, 1992). Although these views were generally held by society for a long time, one can argue that these norms have become somewhat outdated in light of the current shifts in women's rights and personal aspirations. Despite these recent developments, however, many diplomatic accompanying spouses, once referred to as "trailing wives," still confront traditional norms and experience a great amount of pressure to live up to specific expectations. (Shaffer & Harrison, 1998; Shaffer, Harrison, Gilley, Luk 2001).

For these women, expectations from others can be seen as a central factor in their experience as the accompanying spouse of a diplomat. In one of the few studies that deal with spouses of diplomats, Davoine and his colleagues (2012) used Goffman's (2001) dramaturgical approach to explore the social role of spouses of Swiss diplomats during long-term international postings. This study divided the data into three main areas, or repertoire: 1) the spouse gives psychological and/or professional support, and accompanies the diplomat to social events; 2) the spouse represents Switzerland at social events and develops links with the local expatriate community; and 3) the spouse gives administrative support and supervises local staff by becoming a resource manager (Davoine, et. al., 2012). The authors have provided a clear understanding of the complexity of spouses' roles as they conducted their research using an interactionist sociological perspective. This school of thought emphasized different processes of transmitting, sharing social meanings, and developing one's own self through social interactions (Stryker & Vryan, 2006).

Although it is a valuable contribution to the sociological aspect of being an accompanying spouse of diplomat, Davoine and his colleagues' study (2012) did not address the subjective experience of their participants and/or how these role expectations made them feel as accompanying spouses. This lacuna calls for a more subjective experiential exploration of WODs, especially as many researchers expressed concern for the psychological well-being of this group (Arieli, 2007; Bielby & Bielby, 1992; Chiang, 2015; Yellig, 2011).

Davoine and his colleagues (2012) also omitted a crucial part of WOD self-identity, family life. The psychological state of children has been found to be a major stressor for expatriate parents (Arieli, 2007; Ismail, Ali & Shaharudin, 2015), and more specifically for women, who are mainly supporting them emotionally (Arieli, 2007). Different levels of parental involvement result from the fact that diplomats usually enter their professional roles very quickly after arriving in the host country, leading spouses to take care of all the administrative tasks that are related to the transition to the new country (Davoine et al., 2012). This component is not only demanding, but also stressful, as spouses have to help their children integrate themselves into the new community and turn the expatriation experience into a successful endeavor as harmoniously as possible (Franke & Nicholson, 2002).

Arieli (2007) conducted an ethnographic study of 30 Western expatriate wives in Beijing and found that their main source of stress came from the emotional labor necessary to support their husbands and children. Researchers of marriage and family often describe the importance of emotional work that is done for others within the family. Continuously encouraging others, listening and advising, expressing appreciation of and to them, and empathizing with their emotions have been found to be no less important than providing for the children and the household financially (Erickson, 2005).

Given that women tend to do most of the emotional work (Arieli, 2007; Davoine et al., 2012; Erickson, 2005), the implications for their mental health can be serious. Emotional work done for others is both time-consuming and emotionally demanding, and is often unvalued and even belittled, all characteristics that can lead to burnout (Erickson & Ritter, 2001; Haslberger & Brewster, 2008). Additionally, the inequality between husbands and wives with regard to other-centered emotional labor may generate feelings of unsupportiveness toward the women within the marriage, a feeling that has negative effects on her overall well-being (Strazdins & Broom, 2004). As a result, some researchers have concluded that many accompanying spouses encounter great difficulties when becoming WODs as they experience a disruption of social ties and routines, loss of identity and self-worth, loneliness, isolation, and role alteration (Adler, 1986; De Singly & Challand, 2002; Harvey, 1985).

The complexity and irony of WOD's role expectations stand out. Although some studies (Davoine et al., 2012; De Singly & Challand, 2002) have focused on the role of WODs during diplomatic postings, all failed to mention that these expectations were unofficial. Indeed, foreign services are not legally bound to spouses of diplomats in important ways, as they do not officially employ them but still allow their diplomatic representation to take place through the idiom and channel of the family. The wife is thus performing her duties by virtue of her status as a WOD.

This process has had an important effect upon how WODs perceive their senses of duty and diplomatic roles (Hendry & Watson, 2001). Many WODs perceived love and marriage to be a partnership, and accepted that this partnership could spill over into their performing roles in their countries' foreign service (Black, 2001). Although this spillover may seem old-fashioned and outdated, many other countries still retain this theme of dedication with regard to WODs' roles and to the structure within which they work and live. Callan (1975), who was writing at a time of significant flux in attitudes toward gender, introduced the concept of "premise of dedication," a psychological concept that seeks to resolve the paradox of WODs taking on duties that had many salary-like features without being formally employed.

While this short essay represented a shift in the ideology of roles from firm duties and obligations to agency and choice, some associations, such as the British Diplomatic Spouses Association, saw a need to voice these concerns. As a result, the British Foreign Service experienced a change in stance and expressed that "spouses were not expected to do anything in support of the officer but that anything the spouse did on a voluntary basis would be greatly appreciated by the Service" (Black, 2001, p. 264). Some have described this position as derogatory, condescending, and ambiguous (Black, 2001; Hendy, 1998), and it is still the main argument against the idea that spouses should be financially remunerated for their work.

1.3.4 Adjusting to the Identity Threat

Adjusting to cross-cultural moves is a complex process of functioning effectively in a culture other than the one in which a person originally came from (Haslberger, 2005). While the amount of time this process requires is still unclear, some researchers have claimed that adjustment can be achieved within one year (Tung, 1998; Ward et al., 1998), while others found evidence of a longer process which may take up to three years (Bhaskar-Shrinivas, Harrison, Shaffer & Luk, 2005). However, no research has been conducted with regard to diplomatic families and their adjustment levels in multiple relocations.

Individuals who experience diplomatic mobility through expatriation and repatriation deal with new sets of circumstances. The development of acculturation that helps families adjust physically and psychologically is expected to lead to greater harmony between them and their environments throughout the process of relocation. Given that the process of psychological adjustment for diplomats and their families includes a pre-departure period, an expatriation period, and a repatriation period, often experienced repetitively, it is an important element of their experience. Consequently, researchers identified two other strategies of psychological acculturation, namely withdrawal and reaction (Berry, 2003). However, these are often non-viable options that are found to be underlying causes for difficult expatriate assignments (Cieri, Dowling & Taylor, 1991). Moreover, researchers in the fields of cross-cultural psychology highlighted the need to consider separately both the socio-cultural adjustment (being able to fit in a new culture) and the psychological well-being (feelings of satisfaction and well-being), as two different dimensions of cross-cultural adjustment (Searle & Ward, 1990; Ward & Kennedy, 1993).

Using the model of adjustment elaborated by Ward, Okura, Kennedy and Kojima's (1991) as a theoretical basis for expatriation, Black, Mendenhall and Oddou (1998) developed a model of expatriate adjustment. Their model conceptualized expatriation adjustment as a stressful transition experienced along three interrelated dimensions of adjustment: 1) work, 2) interaction, and 3) general adjustments. Given that most WODs are unable to work while on diplomatic postings, they mainly experience the latter two: interaction adjustment (adjustment to interaction with host country nationals and expatriate/diplomatic community) and general adjustment (adjustment to the general cultural and physical environment, such as living conditions, transport, environment, entertainment, food, and shopping). Nonetheless, one can argue that WODs also experience work adjustment as many may take on unofficial roles in the diplomatic mission and participate in diplomatic events and activities. Shaffer and Harrison (2001) have recognized that many antecedents of expatriate employee adjustments have also been applied to accompanying spouses, including personality traits, and perceived organizational and social support. However, some researchers have argued that the adjustment experience of the accompanying wife is both different and more challenging than that of the employed spouse (Adler & Gundersen, 2008).

Shaffer and Harrison (2001) developed a model of expatriate spouse adjustment in which spouses are described as experiencing adjustment in three interrelated dimensions: 1) personal, 2) interactive, and 3) cultural. In order to test their model, they used Black and Stephen's

(1989) measure of cultural and interaction adjustment to operationalize these dimensions, and added a personal adjustment construct to measure the extent to which accompanying spouses made sense of "becoming a part of, belonging to, or feeling at home" in their host countries (Shaffer & Harrison, 2001, p. 239). After interviewing ten accompanying wives living in Hong Kong, Shaffer and Harrison (2001) found that instead of retaining past identities, wives found it more important to establish their new identities by building new interpersonal relationships. However, Mohr and Klein (2004) found another important aspect to add to the adjustment of accompanying wives. In their research, they studied American accompanying wives in Germany and found that along with interaction and cultural adjustment, a third dimension of adjustment was crucial, namely that of role adjustment. Indeed, other researchers have also emphasized the importance of role adjustment to the identity of accompanying spouses in the expatriate experience (Davoine et al., 2012; Cole, 2011; Kupka & Cathro, 2007; McNulty, 2012).

1.4 Relevance to Counseling Psychology

For the past decade, international mobility departments were aware of the danger of neglecting the accompanying spouse of their mobile workforce. The most frequently cited cause of failure in international assignments for expatriates has been the inability for the accompanying spouse to adjust to life abroad (Andreason, 2008; Cartus Corporation, 2014; Cieri, Dowling & Taylor, 1991; NetExpat, 2018; Tung, 1998). A recent significant survey conducted by the Permits Foundation (2018) revealed that spouses are central to the success of international assignments, with 71 percent of corporations agreeing that an unhappy and unintegrated spouse in a host country is the main reason for failed assignments. Although there is no unique definition of a "successful" expatriation (Kraimer & Wayne, 2004), it has been argued that "expatriation is successful if expatriates remain in the assignment until the end of the term, adjust to living conditions in the host country and perform well professionally" (Aycan & Kanungo, 1997, p. 251). It is important, however, to stress that concepts of success and failure are ambivalent terms when used in diplomatic discourse.

With evidence of spillover effects between accompanying spouses and the expatriate employee (Takeuchi, Yun & Tesluk, 2002; van der Zee, Alo & Salome, 2005), spouses appear to be an influential source of either support or stress for the expatriate (Arieli, 2007; Lauring & Selmer, 2010; Lazarova, Westman & Shaffer, 2010). Studies have shown that a spouse's support directly effects the expatriate's adjustment to living conditions in new cultures and indirectly effects his job performances (Kramer, Wayne & Kaworski, 2001; Tung, 1998). Spousal adjustment is therefore an issue of concern in the management of diplomatic relocations.

Nevertheless, the world of research has tended to objectify diplomatic spouses by treating them as "factors" that influence productivity, and have used the economic character of the bargain to mask its emotional side. Some may argue that this phenomenon happens as a result of WODs presenting as women who have resources and high social status primarily through their association with powerful and high-achieving spouse (Reid, et al., 2011), and their exposure to a privileged lifestyle (Arieli, 2007). Indeed, psychology has virtually ignored this minority of women, who are viewed as powerful or privileged perhaps because "their positions appear to many nonintimate observers to be comfortable and even splendid," as explained by sociologist David

Reisman (as cited in Clodius & Magrath, 1984, p. 156). And yet, many wives have made familial, professional, and personal sacrifices in order to support their husbands' careers. Since their contributions are often behind the scenes, their role is often unseen and unvalued by others (Davoine et al., 2012; Domett, 2005; Reid et al., 2011). These women are (unofficially, of course) expected to contribute in major ways to their institutions and communities, often working long hours for little or no pay. As many of these wives arrive in these positions relatively unprepared, they need to rely on public or social opinion to succeed in the work they do on behalf of their husbands and embassies, while being minimized or ignored by the general public and in official discourse.

The concepts of diplomatic mobility and loss of identity have been noted as clearly potent psychological constructs, but have not yet become the subject of systematic research, especially as phenomenological perspectives. A much more thorough investigation into the concept of diplomatic life and WOD experiences is needed, particularly at the subjective level, given that little research interest has been given outside the managerial and human resources fields.

While many questions are still unanswered, this book attempts to explore and provide insight onto this phenomenon. Such questions include: how do WODs maintain their identities when undergoing important changes? How do they operate in their marriages? How are they able to balance their professional and personal needs while meeting others' expectations? How are they able to sustain connections in a highly mobile diplomatic society? How do they manage and cope with the psychological effects of these changes?

I believe that there are particular issues and challenges faced by women married to diplomats, who are regularly expected to portray traditional female roles within a society that increasingly expects women to create and follow their own independent paths. Although feminist research has often focused on women with prestige who have accomplished success in their own right (e.g. Hulbert & Schuster, 1993; Reid & Kelly, 1994), my aim is to give voice to women who, for different reasons, agreed to accompany their husband' on diplomatic assignments.

Additionally, WODs (or their family members) may present at some point for support in different contexts where counseling psychology may be involved (Moore & Rae, 1998), such as education settings, general practitioner offices, assistance programs, and the private sector. The main role of the counseling psychologist is to sit with patients as they try to make sense of who they are in relation to themselves, their world, and others (Kasket, 2012). By working holistically, we can aid others' psychology discipline and our own understand while remaining neutral, non-pathologizing, and non-judgmental (Cooper, 2009).

Chapter 2- Methodology and Procedures[2]

2.1 Overview of Research Design

The research that led to this book used a qualitative research approach, specifically Interpretive Phenomenological Analysis, or IPA (Smith, Flowers & Larkin, 2009). I collected data using semi-structured interviews from a sample of eight Wives of Diplomats (WODs) and then analyzed the data in order to draw out different themes.

2.2 Aims of Research

The aim of this research was to access the experiences of WODs during diplomatic assignments by asking "What is the Experience of Being a Wife of a Diplomat across Diplomatic Assignments?" Throughout this chapter, I reflect upon my choice of research question and methodology by drawing out the role I played in my choices and in the formation of new knowledge. Reflexivity is intertwined throughout this Methodology chapter.

While carrying out my research, I took an exploratory, transparent approach that paralleled the ideals of counseling psychology and IPA. I hope this exploratory approach will generate some understanding of the phenomenon of being a WOD, and that it will encourage others to take an interest in additional research in this overlooked area. Finally, I hope to

---

[2] This chapter was written in the first person in order to express the reflective nature of the research and to address the reader directly when describing the research stages and processes.

help mental health professionals reflect on their clinical work, with an understanding of the experiences of WODs providing additional insights.

2.3 Rationale for using a Qualitative Approach

As a trainee in counseling psychology, I felt that qualitative research resonated well with my professional and personal development, in contrast to my previous experiences using quantitative methodologies. My clinical practice, relating to my clients at an interpersonal depth, seemed distant from the quantitative methodology, and I wished to approach this study's research question from a similar perspective.

My initial literature review indicated a scarcity of psychological research, and more specifically research in counseling psychology, into WODs. Despite the suggestion of some human resources management and international business studies that WODs play a major role in the quality of diplomatic assignments, there was little psychological research. Consequently, this study's investigative nature leaned towards an inductive approach, as opposed to a hypothetical-deductive one (Thomas, 2006). I did not intend to approach my research question in a deductive manner by attempting to establish general principles or laws, or by engaging in a nomothetic approach that would assume a participant's social reality to be external and objective (Burns, 2000). Instead, I regarded social reality as a "creation of individual consciousness, with meaning, and the evaluation of events seen as a personal and subjective construction" (Burns, 2000, p.3). As Smith et. al. (2009) mentioned, the nomothetic approach to psychology tends to limit the involvement of participants and bases their group-level asseverations on statistics, while an idiographic approach regards participants' subjective and complex data naturalistically, making qualitative research a well-founded choice (Marshall, 1986; Morse, 1994).

Although criticized for lacking the accuracy and precision of quantitative research, qualitative research has been able to explore important areas of psychology that were never considered before, such as people's subjective experiences and their meanings. Also, in line with Ponterotto's (2005, p. 13) view, I agree that counseling psychology "is in the midst of a gradual paradigm shift from a primary reliance on quantitative methods to a more balanced reliance on quantitative and qualitative methods," leading us to believe that they can interdependently coexist (Solomon, 1991). Although others may take the view that this approach may lack the rigor of "real science," qualitative research can be both rigorous and scientific. As Giorgi (2009) suggested with regard to phenomenology, this approach represents a different philosophy of science. This difference can be found by the way this nomothetic approach to psychology makes group-level claims based on statistics (Smith et al., 2009), as opposed to an approach that is idiographic, and respects and values participants and their data.

As a result, both my preference for an idiographic approach and my research question have provided me with a rationale for using a qualitative methodology.

2.4 Epistemological Position and Reflexivity

In order to evaluate a study meaningfully, Willig (2013) stated the importance of (1) asking about the knowledge that the methodology aimed to produce, (2) the assumptions that it made about the world and (3) the conceptualization of the researcher's role in the research process.

Willig (2013) explained that there are three types of knowledge a researcher aims to produce: social-constructionist, phenomenological, and/or realist knowledge. Given that my central research question is "How Does the Experience of Being Wives of Diplomats Shape How They Feel About Themselves and Their Relationships Across Diplomatic Assignments?," I aimed to produce phenomenological knowledge, as I wanted to know about the subjective experiences of WODs by getting "as close as possible to the research participant's experience, and enter their experiential world by stepping into their shoes and looking at the world through their eyes" (Willig, 2013, p. 16).

I started by questioning assumptions I had made about the world, predominantly by trying to answer the ontological question of "What is reality?" in relation to human existence, or as Willig (2008, p. 13) put it, "What is there to know?" I do not perceive reality as consisting only of objective sets of facts that can be measured and discovered. While a positivist position sees reality as an objective set of facts that has a "direct correspondence between things and their representation" (Willig, 2013, p. 4), I dispute that a direct cause and effect association exists between them. At the same time, I do not take an extreme relativist position, according to which reality exclusively exists in people's claims of it. Instead, I situate myself between the poles of realism and relativism and take a critical-realist position. I retain an ontological realism that states that there is a real world existing independently of our constructions, theories, and perceptions, and I accept another form of epistemological relativism and constructivism that understands the experiential world as a construction of our own standpoints and perspectives (Maxwell, 2012).

My clinical practice has confirmed my position on this. I realized that some clients' approaches to the world can be unhelpful and self-defeating, and that accepting their realities can help strengthen the therapeutic alliance and eventually move toward change. I believe that participants will interpret in their own way the "reality" of their experiences, as they cannot entirely access this "reality." Therefore, I do not assume that participants' experiences will be directly related to an external "reality," and understand that each will have different experiences of this "reality" depending on their interpretations of it. Moreover, given that we can never be fully aware of this external "reality," I will accept that the data provided during interviews will not be an evident indication of what happens in the "real" world, and that a degree of interpretation will be needed to illuminate the phenomenon of being a WOD.

Nonetheless, I also believe that participants' social contexts have to be imperatively acknowledged within human experience. I take on Coyle's (2007) conceptualization of context as "the social systems and feedback loops in which an individual is embedded and through which they make sense of, construct and are constructed by their worlds" (p. 17). Hence, in agreement with the social constructionist approach, both historical and sociocultural processes play central roles in how we experience and understand our world, and in how we construct and interpret our experiences (Eatough & Smith, 2008; Willig, 2013). Indeed, Eatough and Smith's (2008) position maintains that sociocultural context and discourses influence the way participants tell, understand and give meaning to their stories. I am also influenced by their position on IPA, as I also believe that language is a crucial part of how participants experience their social worlds. Throughout this study, I focused carefully on how

WODs chose to reflect and express their experiences, as "reality is both contingent upon and constrained by the language of one's culture" (Eatough & Smith, 2008, p. 184). On the other hand, Madill, Jordan, and Shirley (2000) suggested that "contextual constructionism" holds knowledge to be situational, provisional, and local; hence, "different perspectives generate different insights into the same phenomenon" (Willig, 2013, p. 172), thereby leading the research to seek completeness instead of accuracy. Finally, Larkin, Watts, and Clifton (2006) concluded that there is a need for phenomenology to engage meaningfully with different aspects of constructionist values, as the phenomenon in question is viewed as occurring in a certain cultural and personal context during a certain time and place.

Therefore, I position myself between critical-realism and contextual-constructionism. I have paid particular attention to cultural influences on meaning and how they entwined with WODs lived experiences.

2.5 IPA Methodology

2.5.1 Overview and Background of IPA

IPA aims to shed light on the detailed personal experiences that participants have of influential life events, exploring how they make sense of their life-world, both social and personal (Smith & Osborn, 2003). Therefore, there is an important emphasis on the meaning that participants make of their experiences.

IPA was first developed by Jonathan Smith (1996) as an intermediary between the positivistic experimental approach to social cognition and the social constructionism of discourse analysis (Smith et al., 2009). IPA aims to explore how individuals make sense of their experiences, by taking an extensive view of their meaning-making, awareness, reflexivity, and hot cognition, both in their social and personal contexts (Smith & Osborn, 2003). By not minimizing and conceptualizing the experience as a theoretically predefined concept, the IPA researcher explores the human experience by looking at the experiential rather than the experimental data. (Eatough & Smith, 2008; Smith et al., 2009). I found IPA to resonate with my own sense of the complexity of cognition and my reluctance to take a polarized approach to epistemology.

In addition, IPA claims to be well suited for the investigation of new topics that are multi-dimensional, contextual, involved in the exploration of sense-making process that are significant to individuals, and concerned with individuals' subjective experiences. As a result, IPA often touches upon issues of self-concept and identity (Smith, 2004).[3]

As the name indicates, IPA is both phenomenological and interpretative. It draws on hermeneutics as its theory of interpretation. It also takes an idiographic approach with a specific focus on the particular. I consider all three philosophical influences below.

2.6 Phenomenology

Langdridge (2007) suggested that phenomenology is a philosophy that studies the in-depth exploration of individuals' lived experiences. It aims to understand how a phenomenon is perceived according to the context and time within an individual's consciousness (Willig, 2013, p. 85). Phenomenology was first initiated by Husserl (1927), who proposed that it was possible "to transcend presuppositions and biases and to

---

[3] For IPA studies that directly explored issues of identity see e.g. Coyle and Rafalin (2000) who explored religious and sexual identity, and Timotijevic and Breakwell (2000) who explored identity threat and immigration.

experience a state of pre-reflective consciousness, which allows us to describe phenomena as they present themselves to us" (Willig, 2013, p. 84). In this context, IPA explores systematically the content of our consciousness by reflecting and processing our understanding of our social and personal experiences (Smith et al., 2009). In his early work, Husserl (1927) suggested that in order to research psychic experiences, one has to acquire a phenomenological attitude, via reflectivity, while stepping out of the natural attitude. He proposed to "bracket" our assumptions about the external world by setting aside what we already know about them (Willig, 2013).

Heidegger reconceived this phenomenological attitude by questioning Husserl's (1927) "return to the things themselves." He explained that as individuals, our meanings are formed through our experience of being in the world (Heidegger, 1962; Spiegelberg, 2012). Byrne (2001, p. 831) suggested that "Heidegger acknowledged that culture, history, and related life experiences prohibit an objective viewpoint." Indeed, Heidegger (1962) challenged the concept of bracketing, for he believed that it is through the scope of our own interpretation that we are truly able to understand and investigate participants' experiences (Smith et al., 2009). Heidegger's approach is one that is similar to mine; I do not feel capable of completely "bracketing" my assumptions, but I can surely question them and make them as transparent as possible to the readers.

2.6.1 Hermeneutics

IPA also draws on hermeneutics (Gadamer, 1975; Heidegger, 1962; Schmidt, 2016). The researchers' role in IPA is one of constant interpretation (Willig, 2013). By acknowledging that Husserl's bracketing can only be reached to some extent, Heidegger (1962) and Gadamer (1975) agreed that to preclude the imposition of meaning based on one's preconceptions, one constantly needs to preserve a reflective openness to biases and prejudices. Consequently, this interpretative process involves a hermeneutic circle (Dilthey, 1976; Heidegger, 1962; Gadamer, 1975; Schleiermacher, 1998). This cyclical process is of great importance in IPA as it allows researchers to intentionally bracket their experiences, and to engage entirely with the participant's own experience. By involving a "back and forth" analytic process, Smith et. al. (2009) argue that a number of various meanings can emerge, as every "understanding requires a circular movement from presupposition to interpretation and back again" (Willig, 2013, p. 86).

Given that IPA endeavors to "know" the participant's world, researchers engage in double-hermeneutic as they try "to make sense of the participants trying to make sense of their world" (Smith & Osborn, 2003, p. 51). During this process, researchers are both interrogative, using psychological theories to shed light on participants' experiences, and empathic, aiming to adopt the participant's perspective (Smith et al., 2009).

2.6.2 Idiography

IPA takes an idiographic approach, as it does not make claims about groups and population, but tries instead to make specific statements about certain individuals (Smith & Osborn, 2003). Smith et. al. (2009) propose that a commitment to idiography in IPA involved the need for in-depth analysis along with the necessity of openness to the unique view that the individual in question can offer of his/her experience of the phenomena. In parallel, they pointed out that phenomenology incorporates the entrenched nature of the contexts that influence the individual's experience. They suggest that the analytic procedures of IPA are also able to sustain an idiographic commitment while developing more general commentaries and themes. Smith et. al. (2009, p. 29) go on to argue that an idiographic approach does not signify that more engraved generalities can never be made in IPA, but that they would develop progressively as more research studies in the specific area are carried out.

2.7 Rationale for IPA

Some methodological approaches were considered prior to choosing IPA, such as Grounded Theory (GT) (Glaser & Strauss, 1967), and Discourse Analysis (DA) (Potter & Wetherell, 1987).

This study aims at taking an exploratory approach to looking at WODs during diplomatic assignments as an undefined new experience. This study does not intend to develop a theory about WODs, but instead seeks to illuminate their experiences by enabling the progress of a tentative model (Smith et al., 2009). As Langdridge and Hagger-Johnson (2009) further suggested, Grounded Theory (GT) leaves out participants' internal worlds, which are a crucial concept for this study, and indeed its main focus.

Although Discourse Analysis (DA) is similar to IPA's commitment to qualitative analysis and language, it differs in its perception of the role of cognition. Potter and Wetherell (1987) explained that the main focus of DA is on the construction, consequences, and functions of discursive organization, and that DA is a "radically non-cognitive form of social psychology" (p. 178). This study, on the other hand, is cognitively driven as it is mainly concerned with the beliefs, internal thoughts and meaning-making processes of the WOD. Smith,

Flowers and Osborn (1997) added that "DA regards verbal reports as behaviours in their own right which should be the focus of functional analyses" (p. 70).

I felt that IPA went hand-in-hand with my epistemological stance because it allows for "epistemological openness" (Larkin et al., 2006). Moreover, according to Smith (2004), IPA has been found to be the most suitable analytic strategy to use when the research explores issues of identity. IPA looks at the individual as a complete and unique entity: it does not reduce or lose the individuality of the participant.

As a methodology, IPA can be rigorously scientific, even though it takes a different point of view from that of quantitative research (also see section 2.8 below). It was chosen for its focus on meaning-making processes and its concern with cognitive psychology. Cognitive psychology has been mainly "dominated by quantitative research anchored in positivist and post-positivist research paradigm" (Ponterotte, 2005, p. 126), although its focus was originally formulated as having "acts of meaning" (Bruner, 1990, p. 3). In return, researchers such as Eathough and Smith (2008) have called for a broader view of cognition and promoted IPA for its analysis of subjective meaning-making processes. They both acknowledged the importance of language in the intersubjective development of the self, although I put less importance on the discursive aspect of language.

2.8 Evaluating Research

Qualitative methodologies are concerned with the validity of their research. Although they are distinct from the reliability and validity of positivistic research (Lyons & Coyle, 2007), Finlay (2006) suggests that there is still a great discrepancy in views on how qualitative studies should be evaluated. As Cho and Trent (2006) proposed, "validity in qualitative research is about determining the degree to which researchers' claims about knowledge correspond to the reality (or research participants' constructions of reality) being studied" (p. 320). However, researchers have encountered limits in attempting to judge validity when using strict criteria to judge research or, on the contrary, use extreme relativist positions (Seale, 1999). Consequently, I followed Lucy Yardley's (2008) proposition for demonstrating validity by showing sensitivity to context, commitment, rigor, coherence, transparency, impact, and importance. In section 4.3 of the Discussion, the quality markers of this research project will be further discussed.

2.8.1 Sensitivity to Context

I attempted throughout the study to achieve sensitivity to context by engaging thoroughly in readings of relevant theoretical and empirical studies in a variety of areas, including psychology, sociology, and international business. During interviews, I also demonstrated sensitivity to participants' perspectives by conducting semi-structured interviews and using, for example, open-ended questions (Stroud, 2015). Moreover, I demonstrated awareness and sensitivity to the sociocultural context within which the experience of WODs took place, and tried to be cognizant of assumptions and points of view as a researcher (see Personal Reflexivity, section 2.9).

2.8.2 Commitment and Rigor

I registered in IPA training seminars and read numerous papers on IPA and philosophical theory. I have also aimed at demonstrating commitment and rigor by engaging my colleagues and supervisor in cross-readings to give feedback (Henwook & Pidgeon, 1992). The feedback I received allowed me to step back from the data, especially when I felt that I was unable to see the bigger picture. Professional feedback thereby helped me reengage in the hermeneutic circle.

Smith et. al. (2009) propose that the research sample should be carefully selected and be as homogeneous as possible. I have tried to show rigor selecting participants. The extant literature presents little knowledge of WODs, which made it difficult for me to justify the recruitment of WODs belonging to a certain age or ethnicity group. To be sensitive to the paucity of knowledge, I felt that I had to be rigorous in aiding the self-selection of the sample without limiting the inclusion criteria. Consequently, I consciously courted a sample that would allow WODs of any experience to assist their husbands across diplomatic assignments to come forward (see section 2.10.1).

While conducting the analysis, I used negative case analysis (Lincoln & Guba, 1985). As preliminary themes started to emerge, I looked for participants' experiences that were antithetical, with the aim of refining the analysis until it explained and accounted for the majority of cases. I went through repeated cycles of abandoning, adjusting, and expanding themes, until I was able to confirm the different patterns emerging from the data (Patton, 2001).

I aimed to develop an analysis and interpretation that has enough insight and depth to add to WOD research. I tried to develop an empathic understanding of my participants' experiences while taking into consideration their sociocultural context. I grounded and re-grounded my findings and interpretations in their experiences, with the aim of staying as close to the data as possible.

2.8.3 Transparency and Coherence

In section 2.10, I describe how I selected the participants and developed my interview schedule, and discussed my approach to the analysis and write-up. By doing this, I aimed to make the research process as transparent as possible. Additionally, I engaged in personal reflection and kept a research diary in order to clarify how my experiences and thought processes as a researcher were unavoidably part of the research process, and discussed my involvement double-hermeneutic processes. I also aimed to achieve coherence and transparency by including participants' own words.

Throughout this research process, I kept all of my notes concerning my developing ideas about my topic, my post-interview and transcription comments, and my notes concerning the development of the themes, as Smith et. al. (2009) suggested. These notes, alongside my corrected drafts, have been points of reference to check the coherence and progression of my thoughts. The final arbiter of the coherence of this book, however, will of course be the reader.

2.8.4 Impact and Importance

Yardley (2008) explains that an important vessel for good quality qualitative research is the effect and significance of what this new knowledge presents. I have aspired to select a challenging topic that has been little researched, especially in psychology, and which has potential significance for the many women who follow and assist their spouses in foreign countries. I expand on this in greater depth when considering the relevance of my findings for counseling psychology.

2.9 Personal Reflexivity

This section was written after interviewing participants. In the Discussion Chapter, I will further consider personal reflexivity following the analysis.

Willig (2013, p. 10) describes personal reflexivity as a useful point to start when considering the research project: "Personal reflexivity involves reflecting upon the ways in which our own values, experiences, interests, beliefs, political commitments, wider aims in life and social identities have shaped the research. It also involves thinking about how researchers shape the ongoing research and how the research may have affected and possibly changed us, as people and as researchers."

In order for the reader to assess how this study contributes to knowledge, I feel it is important to state my position as a researcher clearly (Marshall, 1986; Willig, 2013). My personal interest in this specific topic is two-fold. First, as a young child, I was always charmed by WODs who visited our house, two of whom, in particular, enhanced my fascination with their lifestyle. Their elegance and ability to make conversation seemingly with anyone captivated me and made me want to become one of them, an infantile desire that I outgrew during my teenage years. In my early twenties, my fantasy of WODs lives took a turn when I met my fiancé's mother, a WOD herself. After sharing my one-sided fascination of what one could accomplish through multiple expatriations, she was kind enough to share her own difficult personal experience of being a WOD and the different obstacles she faced throughout her journey.

Second, my parents have always encouraged me to build a strong and independent identity as a woman, while at the same time conforming to conservative family and cultural traditions. These conflicting stances have affected my views on women's identities and abilities to become their fullest selves. Indeed, although I was partly raised to have feminist values, my views on women's happiness became defined by their ability to realize personal achievements and reach their maximum potential while being valued and appreciated for the individuals they became. I now understand that the way I understand the world in which I live may have been influenced by my experience of being surrounded by women whose time and efforts were undervalued and rarely appreciated, engendering an intense sense of injustice and inability to accept unfairness. Upon reflection, I also recognize that my personal views and interest in WODs may have stemmed from a place of similar emotions where, inequality and negligence were being experienced, inflaming in me the need to give them a voice.

My period of reflection around WODs helped me realize that their experiences deserved greater psychological attention from an academic perspective. Nonetheless, I quickly realized that my own anecdotal experiences and personal attitudes about WODs' experiences were going to influence my research. I understood that given my strong feelings and assumptions, a significant need for reflection was indispensable. To this end, I began a research diary in which I wrote my thoughts and feelings with regard to my topic, and reflected on the different ways in which they may have influenced my interpretations of the study. I also became transparent with my supervisors by sharing my views on WODs and allowing them to challenge these assumptions.

Although I have chosen WODs as an area of research, I tried my best to maintain a stance of curiosity while writing the interview schedule, conducting the interviews, analyzing the data, and discussing the findings.

I am aware now, in a way that I was not before supervision and the write-up, that I do not want to fall into the role of social advocate for WODs. Undeniably, there were times when I felt that I was taking the role of social advocate as I became defensive when friends or colleagues would challenge me about the topic. I have tried to manage these issues by expanding my awareness as much as possible with regard to WODs and their experiences. My awareness of how my own assumptions, experiences, and materials may have influenced and directed the research process has been at the center of my own reflexivity. This is because I felt that the more I became aware of my own processes, the more I would be able to bracket my knowledge and assumptions. As mentioned, this was partly achieved through the use of supervision and my research diary.

While reflecting on my own assumptions, I started thinking about my role as a researcher in light of the double-hermeneutic process (Smith & Osborn, 2003). As a researcher, I have had to make sense of my participants' sense-making and cannot remain apart from it. I am reminded of Bunge (1993), who suggested that in the critical-realist epistemological approach, our perception of facts is affected by our attitudes and beliefs, and therefore subjectivity is an important part of understanding and producing knowledge, which will always require personal reflection. This subjectivity is also a result of my professional identity as a trainee counseling psychologist, which allowed me understand WODs' experiences through this professional lens. Reflecting on my interviews, I can say that this lens has shaped my attitude towards my participants and the relationship that we developed during interviews. It also engendered psychological insight, which needed to be put aside in order to allow my participants' voices to be heard. Upon reflection, I notice that my professional background allowed me to make certain assumptions about my participants' experiences, with some that I am probably not aware of. Although bracketing has been recognized as imperfect (Fischer, 2009), I hope that I was able to put aside my own beliefs and feelings, and allow the phenomenon in question to speak for itself (Pietkiewicz & Smith, 2014).

2.10 Data Collection

2.10.1 Sampling

Because of its qualitative nature and idiography, IPA uses small samples; hence, it makes little sense to discuss random sampling and representativeness in the same way a quantitative study would.

IPA recommends the gathering of quality information to generate a deeper understanding of participants' experiences (Clarke, 2009). As a result, Smith et. al. (2009) explain that researchers should aim to recruit a homogeneous sample that represents the area of study. Smith and Osborn (2003) and Yardley (2008) propose that by recruiting a homogeneous sample, the researcher is limiting some of the variations between participants that may emerge in other ways than the one suggested by the research question.

The issue of homogeneity vexed me. I understood that WODs constitute a minority, which narrowed down the pool in selecting research participants. This population qualified as "hard-to-reach," and made it arduous to recruit a sample that had little variation. However, when trying to find different ways of making my sample more homogeneous, I also realized that I was confronting my own initial ideological stance. I found it unjustifiable to privilege a certain group of WODs, or to prevent any participant the opportunity to come forward and to share her experience.

Instead, I decided to give space for any WOD who wanted to say something about her experience to come forward. I am not suggesting that this sample is representative of all WODs, as it was self-selected and rather small. Nonetheless, it will still allow the study to shed light on the wider context and not limit the ability to make associations and transferability (Smith et al., 2009).

By drawing from a broad pool of participants and keeping the research question open, a more heterogeneous sample was created than in most IPA studies. I am reminded of Smith et. al. (2009), who explained that the final measure of the effectiveness of an IPA research project is the amount of light that has been shed on the wider context. I now realize that a more homogeneous sample would have explored only one side of the subject matter and limited the reader's ability to make different connections, an element that Smith et. al. (2009) suggest is important in IPA.

Following the recommendations for professional doctorate sample sizes for IPA, I recruited eight WODs (Smith et. al., 2009). I posted an advertisement on a Facebook group seeking WODs over the age of 18 who are willing to take part in an interview about their experiences of being a WOD. Moreover, two points of contacts helped me recruit participants in Beirut and London (see section 2.11.1).

2.10.2 Semi-Structured Interviews

When settling on the data collection method, my main goal was to choose a method that would engender the most detailed and in-depth data regarding participants' personal experiences. My decision was mainly influenced by Brocki and Wearden (2006), who suggested that IPA researchers should think prudently about the pros and cons of different data collection methods. Indeed, I chose a method that would permit participants to associate information that they considered to be important aspects of their experience. I therefore rejected the use of more structured approaches, such as questionnaires, the rigidity of which tends to constrict data collection and impose prejudgments about participants' experiences. I also rejected diaries, as I wanted to collect data over a longer period of time. I considered the use of personal accounts, but felt that they might disadvantage some participants or put off others.

I decided to use interviews, which allow for discussion, building a rapport, and eliciting novel areas (Smith & Osborn, 2008). This method went hand-in-hand with my skills as a counseling psychologist, relying on my interpersonal communication skills and ability to build rapport in order to gather data (Hargie, 1997). A single interview was a pragmatic and achievable choice, given the time constraints of the research project. This method of data collection allowed me to take notes of non-verbal communication during, after, and while transcribing the interview in order to enrich the analysis. The design of these interviews was semi-structured, as I hoped it would help participants to recall important experiences, allow new concepts to emerge (Dearnley, 2005), and help me pinpoint relevant meanings (Reid, Flowers & Larkin, 2005).

2.10.3 Preliminary Interview Schedule

My preliminary interview schedule comprised a series of questions covering different areas of experience in being a WOD. These initial questions emerged from a multidisciplinary review of WODs as little peer-reviewed psychological research was available. My interview schedule was guided by my research question (Smith & Osborn, 2003). I aimed at scripting the question by using language that could be clearly understood in an interview context (Smith et al., 2009).

At this stage, I engaged in a reflexive interview, by trying to put myself in the WOD's shoes, and recorded the interview. This exercise helped me reflect further on my role as a researcher and guided a reappraisal of the interview schedule. In fact, when I listened to my responses on the audio-recorder, I became aware that some of my questions were not in line with my epistemological stance. I noticed that many prompts were not grounded in my research question and were formulated using close-ended questioning, inadvertently resulting in a paradigm shift by taking a positivist approach. As I considered this more, I felt that my initial interview schedule was incongruent given its incoherence with phenomenological exploration, and that many questions were too directive and held an agenda. I also noticed that in order to get rich and deep data, participants needed to connect emotionally and meaningfully with the specific experience that they were recalling. Therefore, I reworked my interview schedule by reminding myself that IPA looks for the richest and most detailed data and aims to ask open and explorative questions in order to gain depth and breadth (Smith et al., 2009). I realized that having questions focusing on WODs' first diplomatic assignment might explore areas of experience that would engender contrasts and comparisons with later diplomatic assignments.

Despite doing this, I was devoted to using this interview more as an aide-mémoire rather than as a means of inflexibly structuring the interviews according to a certain format. This revised interview schedule was then used for a pilot study.

2.10.4 Pilot Interview and Revision to the Interview Schedule

I decided to undertake a pilot interview in order to get comfortable with the questions and determine whether the interview schedule was well constructed. I was keen to gain feedback on my interviewing style, and to see if the interviewee felt that her experience had been fully explored.

My fiancé's mother, who had taken an interest in the research, volunteered to take part in the pilot interview. She was a WOD herself and therefore fit all the research sampling criteria. I followed the pre-interview, consent and post-interview procedures as closely as possible, in order to rehearse for the actual interview.

I received positive feedback from the pilot participant. I reviewed the data and felt that both depth and breadth were realized, although I had failed to "go deeper" during some part of the interview. I resolved that if opportunities to "go deeper" arose during interviews, I would make use of the prompt, "Can you tell me more about …" in order to elicit further details. My pilot participant reported that the interview had triggered her to think about other areas of her experience, such as being away from her family and how it related to her experience of being a WOD. From this, I made additional changes to the interview schedule.

2.11 Procedure

2.11.1 Recruitment

The research for this book relied upon a convenience sampling technique and selected participants from London and Beirut, given their accessibility and proximity to me. Participants were selected and recruited via two recruitment strategies. First, a flyer was posted on Diplomatic Spouses' Association of Lebanon's Facebook group. Second, participants were selected and recruited through the snowball technique as an informal way to recruit a hard-to-reach population. Two family friends helped recruit participants. One is a WOD herself, and the other the wife of a politician who has many friends in diplomatic service. This method was used one month after posting the ad on Facebook and yielded sufficient responses. Hence, I decided to remove the Facebook ad once all eight participants were recruited. To ensure a random sample, participants were selected in the order to which they had responded.

Two participants heard about the study through one of the points of contact and contacted me. Both participants asked me about the interview questions, expressing a worry that it may get too personal. I replied by writing to outline my main questions and explained that they could skip any question they felt uncomfortable answering. After a week, both participants replied saying that they did not feel ready to share their experiences as WODs, with one specifying that it was "mentally too hard at the moment" for her to do so. I replied thanked them for considering participating and focused on those WODs who had agreed.

2.11.2 Initial Telephone Contact

The advertisement included both my e-mail address and a telephone number dedicated for research, with an invitation to respond by voice or text message. I asked my two points of contact to give the same contact information to any potential participant interested in taking part in the study. When potential participants made a telephone contact, I followed a prepared telephone schedule, which was designed to provide additional information about the study to allow respondents to decide if they wished to participate further. At the end of this initial contact, I sent the interested WODs a "Participant Information Sheet" by e-mail. This allowed participants to access the written information outlining the study, helping them make an informed and considered decision.

2.11.3 Pre-Interview Discussion

For all eight participants, interviews were conducted in their respective homes (see Section 2.12.1 for how I addressed the risk of conducting interviews in participants' homes). Upon meeting participants, and after checking that they were comfortable with starting the interview, I introduced myself, explained the outline of the interview, and provided time to answer any questions they had. Some of them asked for the duration of the interview and how confidentiality would be maintained. Given that the report was to be published, I emphasized that their names would be replaced with a pseudonym and that any identifying details, such as their home countries, would similarly be altered in the research project, in order for their anonymity to be kept at all time. I explained that I allowed time at the end of the interview to debrief, during which we would discuss how the interview felt for them. Following this information, I gave a consent form to participants for them to read and sign. I also gave them a signed copy to retain.

2.11.4 Background Demographic Information Form

After signing the consent forms and before starting the interview, I invited participants to complete a background demographic information form. The aim of this form was to give the reader of the study an idea about the different demographic backgrounds, so that he/she could contextualize the sample. In order to be as transparent as possible about the various backgrounds of participants, I included numerous questions based on the literature review of material pertaining to WODs. These included inquiries about age, ethnic origin, relationship status, number of children, education, and employment. I tried to assure the completion of the form separate from the interview, but in some parts the form became a trigger for different experiences leading participants to such statements as "my two children suffered enormously from this." This valuable data was difficult to develop further on, especially with the first participants, as I wanted to follow the flow of the interview schedule. However, the more I practiced my interview skills with successive participants, the more I found myself being able to leave the form incomplete, explore their shared information, and ask for more details.

2.11.5 Interview

The duration of interviews ranged from approximately one to three hours, with the average lasting one hour and forty-five minutes. Each interview was recorded on a DictoPro digital voice recorder, with data being transferred onto a flash drive and stored in a locked drawer at home. Once the evaluation and appraisal of the study was completed, I destroyed the recorded material.

Adopting an open and relaxed attitude when meeting each participant, while at the same time showing that I was conducting the study in a thoughtful manner, resulted in a pleasant build-up of rapport. The fact that I was referred to each participant by a friend in common also facilitated the relationship. Since the interviews took place in private residences, participants made me feel very welcome by offering a drink and/or some sweets, which made the interview process less formal.

Starting the interview by asking participants their reasons for participation turned out to be an easy question to answer and formed the basis for the rest of the interviews. In the first interview, I found myself slightly stilted at the beginning, as I was trying to stick as much as possible to the interview schedule, without forgetting any prompts. However, in the following interviews, my confidence grew and my ability to interview participants became more natural. I was able to "go with the flow" of each interview and revisit points previously mentioned in a more flexible manner. Although each interview took a different form, most participants found it difficult to stay grounded in their first diplomatic assignments, and instead shifted from one assignment to another. In my initial interviews, I tried to re-ground participants in their first assignments, as I was reminded of the usefulness of staying connected to a specific moment. By re-grounding them, I realized that I was interfering with their views and experiences of having had multiple diplomatic assignments. My flexibility allowed me to understand the usefulness of dipping in and out of their timeframe with regard to their respective experiences. This back-and-forth often helped them make sense of their experiences and roles throughout diplomatic assignments, and I felt it was my ethical responsibility to respect this, as my questions made them realize things about their experiences of which they had not been fully aware in the past.

Before some interviews, some participants asked me how they could prepare for the interview. I was careful to explain that the research is about their personal experiences and that no preparation was necessary. I also noticed that during some interviews, participants asked whether they were giving me "useful" information, and even sometimes became apologetic for not having had "really bad experiences" that they could report. These comments positioned me in the role of an expert seeking to find only the bad aspects of being a WOD, which was not what I intended.

In my first interviews, I referred to the interview schedule as a checklist, in order to ensure that I had not missed any areas that I wanted to cover. I found this process quite stressful and unnatural, as it prevented me from concentrating fully with the participant. As a result, I decided by the third interview to memorize my interview schedule and leave it in a folder in case I needed to monitor the coverage of different topics (Smith & Osborn, 2008). Keeping in mind that I wanted to guide and facilitate the interview, rather than dictate exactly what would happen, I found that by memorizing the interview schedule, I was able to refer to it only as an indicator of the general topics of interest and use it to help provide cues if my participants were having difficulties.

2.11.6 Post-Interview Debrief

After each interview, I conducted a verbal debrief with each participant, asking how she felt about the interview and inviting additional questions. All participants responded that they had enjoyed the interview, describing it as a positive opportunity to reflect on their lives and journeys as WODs. Some remarked that they had forgotten how much their lives felt like a rollercoaster and that they were proud of themselves for having overcome many obstacles. Others shared their feelings in regards to their children, suggesting that I should also conduct a research project on children of diplomats. After receiving their feedback on the interview, a resource pack was provided to all participants, explaining that if the interview negatively affected them, mental health support services were available should they want to receive psychological support.

After answering their questions, I thanked the participants and turned off the digital voice recorder. At the beginning of each interview, participants expressed an interest in getting to know me and to understand how I was related to the person who had referred them. They were appreciative of the fact that I was mainly here for the interview, but still expressed an interest of talking more "when the interview is over." My understanding of this particular interest was one that I formulated as *formal vs. informal* conversation. I felt it was only natural for me to end any formalities in order to have an "off-the-record" conversation, during which many participants offered me refreshments and gave me a tour of their diplomatic residences.

This gesture was very much appreciated by participants, as many verbal and non-verbal cues suggested the possibility for a relaxed heart-to-heart conversation. At this moment, all participants asked questions about my interest in this topic and how it had developed, which I was happy to share. Three of the participants offered help in recruiting more participants, with one calling a friend while I was still in the house. Two others shared information about associations dedicated to spouses of diplomats. Three participants felt comfortable enough to disclose some personal problems they were having in regards to their children's education and accommodation. All three asked for my professional opinion as a trainee counseling psychologist, and for my academic opinion as an alumna of different universities. One of the participants offered me a book she had written, suggesting that it would help me understand her experience further. Two participants introduced me to their husbands and explained what my research project was about. Both husbands shared their opinion of WODs and the positive role they play in diplomatic assignments. Finally, while leaving their homes, five participants confided very personal information about the effect of their assignments on their mental health, suggesting that some cried regularly and that others had doubts about their husbands' fidelity (see Section 4.2.2). After validating their feelings, these participants were reminded of the different ways they could ask for help and seek psychological support.

2.11.7 Post-Interview Reflexivity

After the completion of each interview, I wrote notes on the participants' reactions, what they evoked, and the effect the interview had on me. My notes also documented my thought processes and a summary of my initial impressions of them. Most importantly, I tried to write verbatim what some participants had told me after the recorder went off, as much of the information was very important for fully understanding their experiences. I was aware of my inability to use this data in my analysis, but felt that the experience of disclosure when turning off the recorder was important to note and reflect upon. I also made notes of the two husbands whom I had met and the comments they made about WODs. I treated each set of interview and post-interview notes as part of my learning process. During the analysis and write-up, I revisited my notes in order to reflect further on my emerging understanding, and used our experience of formal vs. informal conversation in the Discussion chapter. Any ethical concerns that arose from interviews were handled appropriately and were documented in my notes.

2.11.8 Transcription

I used Microsoft Word to transcribe each interview verbatim. I transferred each interview onto my computer and used iTunes to listen to the recordings, as it was easier to use the play, rewind, and fast-forward buttons on the computer than on the device itself. I aimed at keeping a level of detail in the transcriptions that would significantly reflect the interview. It was made at the semantic level and included notes of non-verbal communication and pauses. In order to keep the data as rich and as close to the text as possible, the transcribed interviews were left intact despite any inconsistencies in the participants' speech. Wide margins were also left on both sides of the document for analytic commentary, and each line was numbered. Every interview was deleted from my computer and removed from the "Recently Added" folder on iTunes once the transcription was completed.

2.11.9 Analysis of Data

As I started the analysis stage, I was aware that I was inevitably part of the research process, and that I would need to ensure reflexivity in order for the analysis to remain grounded in the data. In IPA, interpretations have been described as involving a "double hermeneutic" character as I aimed to make sense of my participants' sense making (Smith & Osborn, 2003, p. 53). The aim of this analysis was to move from the particulars of one participant's experience to shared experiences among all eight participants. This process of analysis involved numerous iterations, as every transcript was analyzed one-by-one and emergent themes were gradually grouped into superordinate themes. The process was repeated across all participants' superordinate themes, which eventually developed into a set of master themes. These master themes attempted to capture the essence of shared experience while at the same time allowing for some divergence to remain. My description below of these different stages seems to overly simplify the process and makes it sound as one that was straightforward. In reality, however, this process has been complex, repetitive, and convoluted. Initial coding and emergent themes were explored multiple times in an attempt to ensure that they were representative of the participants' accounts. Although I consider these findings to be only one of many possibilities, I am reminded of Reid et. al.

(2005), who pointed out that what is truly important is for the analysis to be plausible to those who read it.

2.11.9.1 Reading the Transcripts

The first stage of the analysis started by reviewing in detail at one interview at a time before analyzing further interviews in order to build-up the master themes (Smith & Osborn, 2008). The first interview was chosen on the basis of the participant's rich explanation of her experience. I decided to analyze each interview immediately after transcribing it, as the interview and the participant felt quite vivid in my memory at the time.

2.11.9.2 Initial Notes

After transcribing an interview, I re-read the text twice alongside the audio recordings in order to familiarize myself with the interview further. I also read and reflected upon my initial impressions recorded during and after the interviews. With each reading, I made initial notes about my impressions, insights, and ideas on the right-side margin as I read through it line by line. At this stage, I engaged in microcodings as I aimed to annotate each line, while staying as close to the text as possible. With further readings, I started adding linguistic and conceptual comments, using different colors to distinguish them (Willig, 2013). These comments brought a new layer of richness to my codings, which allowed me to see the text through a deeper lens. There were times when I felt that my coding became more abstract, sometimes as a result of my inability to focus further. When this happened, I returned to them the following day and changed, extended, or rejected the coding with a new one that felt more grounded in the transcript.

2.11.9.3 Developing themes

While making notes in the left-side margin, I read through the interviews again in order to develop some emergent themes that would capture some of the essence of the initial coding I made prior to this stage. In order to find my emergent theme, I would read my initial coding from the right-side margin and ask such questions as, "What is X experienced as?'" or "What is X an experience of?" The answers would become my emergent themes that I then annotated on the left side.

Although at this stage my emergent themes were still grounded in the text, their meaning increased in profundity (see Table 1 for an example of how themes evolved). Once all emergent themes had been annotated on the left-side margin, I created a Word document in which I wrote each emergent theme in one column, the quote that represents it in another column, and the participant pseudonym, and page and line numbers in a third column. After printing the emergent themes, I cut every row into vignettes in order to maneuver the cross-linking and creation of subthemes. I found this means of manipulating data helpful to move and reform themes.

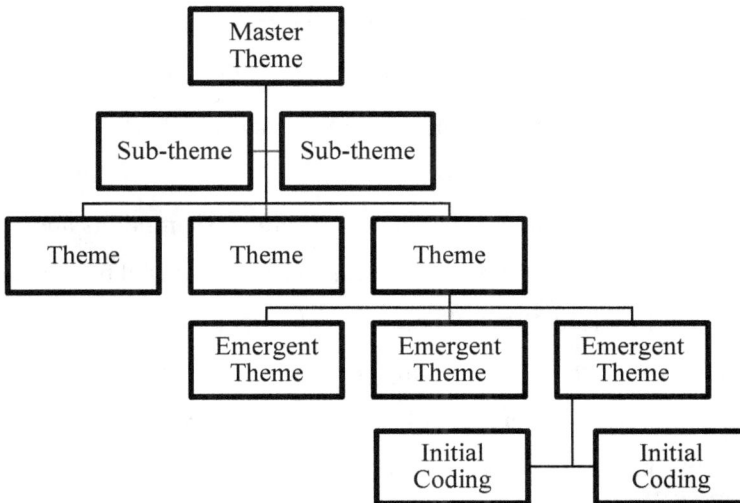

Table 1: Development of Themes

2.11.9.4 Cross-linking of themes

In this stage, Smith and Osborn (2008) explain that emergent themes need to cluster into themes. To facilitate the process, I used vignettes in order to cross-link emergent themes and create clustered themes, which were checked for meaning against the transcripts. Smith and Osborn (2003, p. 70) used the idea of magnets in order to imagine how some emergent themes would tend to coalesce as the researcher attempts to make sense of the data. Using vignettes to create themes helped me sense the connection between different emergent themes and subsume them into other themes. When the clustering process plateaued, the emergent themes became themes and different subthemes were listed above them. For each participant, a summary table was then created including sub-themes, themes, emergent themes, quotations, and their location in the text.

2.11.9.5 Selection of the next participant for analysis

As I analyzed new transcripts, I found that my "fore-structures" had been affected by my previous analyses and that I was unavoidably influenced to some extent. Nonetheless, by meticulously following the steps in the procedure and reflecting on different assumptions about what might succeed, I understood that rather than being imposed by themes that had emerged before, new themes could eventually emerge in later transcripts. In order to evaluate my themes, I brought a segment of my analyzed transcript with a table of themes to my peers and asked them to review my material for plausibility. Although this process did not constitute validation by triangulation (Madill et al., 2000), I found it useful as time was spent exploring my choices of themes and understanding my participants' experiences. My themes were further reviewed with my research supervisor. At this stage of the analysis, I had between four and five master themes for each participant.

2.11.9.6 Developing themes across participants

Once every transcript had been analyzed, it was time to develop the themes across participants. All sub-themes were compared across participants using the same procedure of clustering as described above. Vignettes of the themes had been printed out in order to carry the work on a table. When a master theme had been recognized, I engaged in a back-and-forth checking between the name of the master theme, the themes that depicted it, the transcripts and the quotes that had been incorporated into it. The analysis continued until "saturation" had been reached and no themes could be further integrated, as suggested by Willig (2013). I then assembled a table of master themes and sub-themes together with the quotations that best represented them. This table was used as the foundation of the write-up process of the Analysis chapter (Chapter 3 below). During the write-up, the structure and names of the themes were reworked as a result of laying the table into an analytical text.

2.12 Ethical considerations

The research for this book was subject to approval granted by the Ethics Committee of the Department of Psychology at City, University of London. Because this research was conducted in both the United Kingdom and Lebanon, it received insurance cover approval. Throughout, I prioritized the consideration of ethics at every stage. My two main concerns were to protect the participants from any harm the research could have inflicted on them, and to secure their confidentiality throughout the interview process and write-up. Other concerns included participants' informed consent and right to withdraw from the study, while conducting the project in a way that preserved respect towards each participant and avoided judgment. These points are discussed further below.

2.12.1 Throughout design and implementation

As an ethical consideration, respect towards participants underlined this study in an indispensable way. I reflected on the extant literature on WODs and the ways in which they are perceived in society. I aimed to respect all participants' experiences of what it means to be a WOD and to avoid any prejudicing aspect of their sense-making by keeping the research question as open as possible and not focusing on any single aspect of their experience. I maintained this stance throughout the analysis of interviews and during the writing stage.

Not offering any financial inducement for taking part in the research was a decision I took based on motivational factors. I did not want any financial incentives to become a possible motivation for taking part in the research, for I hoped that each participant would participate on the basis of wanting to willingly share their experiences. Moreover, I felt that offering a financial inducement would become problematic if a participant wanted to withdraw from the study later.

In order to avoid causing harm to participants, I considered designing the research in a way that would involve no more psychological and physical risk to participants than the day-to-day risks they experience. Given the potentially sensitive nature of the research topic, however, I reflected on the possibility that some participants might find the interview process more difficult than I could anticipate. In order to remain sensitive to this possibility, I conducted interviews in a flexible manner, allowing each WOD to take the lead on what they felt needed to be discussed. I also remained sensitive by paying attention to verbal and non-verbal cues that suggested their reluctance to discuss further certain delicate areas.

Before starting each interview, I engaged in a pre-interview discussion with participants based on their understanding of the research. I asked participants if they had any queries before starting the interview and reminded them of their right to skip any question if they felt uncomfortable answering. I felt it was important to minimize the potential for harm by helping them understand that I was putting their personal and psychological interest before my academic one. When participants expressed the wish to continue their interviews, I asked them to sign consent forms. I highlighted the most important points of the form by reminding them that the interview was being audio-recorded, and of their right to withdraw from the study prior to the analysis stage.

During the interviews, I tentatively used the schedule to prompt additional experiences, letting participants know that they may find some questions irrelevant or too personal. Importantly, I allowed for a post-interview debrief in which participants and I were able to discuss the interviews and any difficulties that may have risen. During debrief, most participants expressed how proud they were of their journeys and their ability to overcome obstacles. Some participants expressed additional worries in regards to their children and their futures. I paid particular attention to these debriefs to ensure that the participants felt grounded before I left their home. I also engaged in an off-the-record debrief with each participant. This debrief proved to be very useful as the simple gesture of turning off the audio-recorder engendered deeper conversations (See Discussion Chapter). Any ethical considerations that arose from these conversations were taken care of in a similar manner as the ones brought up on-record. I had prepared a debrief information pack for each participant. Two debrief information packs were prepared, given that the interviews took place both in Lebanon and London. Participants were given the appropriate pack as it contained contact numbers of mental health organizations that might prove helpful should any participant experience distress at a later stage.

I also paid attention to my own self-care. Given that interviews took place in participants' private residences, I was aware that I was entering the homes of people who were essentially strangers to me. This situation carried some potential risk, should a participant have the intention to harm me or my comfort levels. Although this was seen as a risk, it was outweighed by the potential benefits of the study once I had put the right precautions in place. Since participants were referred through two close personal contacts, I trusted their judgment with regard to the participants. I also put in a place a "buddy system," which included a close friend or parent who was made aware of the timing and location of my interviews. I contacted them prior to my interview, advised them of its approximate duration, and indicated that I would contact them against afterward. If I had failed to contact them at the intended hour, they had a prearranged procedure to follow. Predictably, no harm was caused by any participant and the interviews proceeded in the safest environments.

One of my main concerns was to ensure the anonymity of the participants. All identifiable personal materials have remained confidential as they were altered. A pseudonym was given to participants while transcribing and referring to them in the Analysis chapter. Other details, such as their nationalities and the countries of their diplomatic assignments, were also altered, mainly in the Analysis Chapter below. I intended to write case summaries for every participant, allowing the reader to grasp an idea of the participants' lives and contexts. However, this felt like a breach of confidentiality as the diplomatic community is rather small and participants could be recognized, even if their information was altered. Hence, I decided to exclude case summaries in order to protect anonymity. Also, the transcripts were kept on a password-protected computer in my home to which only I had access. Recordings, my research diary, analyzed transcripts, vignettes, consent forms, and the demographics sheets were all kept in a locked filing cabinet in my home.

2.12.2 Write-up

While writing this book and the project on which it was based, I was aware of the necessity of organically engaging with the data to allow meanings emerge, as it is a prerequisite to my methodological and ethical stance. I am reminded of Willig and Stainton-Rogers' (2008) views about imposing meaning on participants' accounts. Throughout this study, I reflected in my research diary on how meanings emerge from the data and my role in this process. When analyzing and discussing the data in the chapters below, I stayed aware that the 'I' in IPA is for Interpretations. I tentatively aimed to reveal another exploratory layer of meaning, while keeping my participants' voices in mind. I attempted to test the developing meanings by always putting myself in my participants' shoes, as though they were reading this study.

Chapter 3 - Findings

This chapter describes the themes and sub-themes that emerged from the interviews, through Interpretative Phenomenological Analysis (IPA). These came about from reaching *gestalt*, a point where I felt the master themes answered the central research question: What is the experience of WODs across diplomatic assignments? In an attempt at presenting a glimpse into these women's experiences, I will use their own words as illustrations.

The respondents who were interviewed were WODs ranging between 46 and 78 years of age. There was no requirement for participants to have English as a native language, but all demonstrated high degree of fluency, including those participants for whom English was their second or third language. A summary of participants' demographic details is set out (pseudonymously) in Table 2 below.

	Age Range	Nationality	Husband Current Diplomatic Status	Education	Previous Employment	Current Employment	Number of Diplomatic Postings	Number of Children and Age Range
Elan	[40-50]	South Asian	Working	Undergraduate Degree	Full Time	Not Working	4	Two [10-20]
Marta	[50-60]	South American	Working	Post-Graduate Degree	Full Time	Freelancing	5	Two [20-40]
Sarah	[40-50]	European	Working	Post-Graduate Degree	Full Time	Not Working	2	No Children
Caline	[50-60]	Middle Eastern	Working	Post-Graduate Degree	Full Time	Not Working	3	Two [10-20]
Lina	[50-60]	Middle Eastern	Retired	Undergraduate Degree	Full Time	Not Working	3	Three [20-30]
Amy	[50-60]	Middle Eastern	Retired	Post-Graduate Degree	Full Time	Not Working	3	Three [10-20]
Ava	[50-60]	European	Working	Post-Graduate Degree	Full Time	Not Working	6	Two [20-30]
Louise	[70-80]	European	Retired	No University Degree	Full Time	Freelancing	9	Two [40-50]

Table 2: Participants Demographic Details

I decided to avoid referring to theory throughout this chapter, as I wanted it to represent a close reflection of my participants' voices. I wanted this chapter to focus mainly on their lived experiences, rather than risk them being shadowed by the theoretical discussion. As a result, I will discuss the findings in light of theory in the chapter following the analysis.

The themes that have emerged from these interviews have been clustered into four master themes, which are then divided into sub-themes. A brief outline of the Master Theme is set out in Figure 1.

1.   **Power of Marriage**
1.1.   Love
1.2.   Togetherness
1.3.   Emotional Support
2.   **Loss of Self**
2.1.   This is Not About Me
2.2.   Loss of Agency
2.3.   Wasted Intellectual Potential
2.4.   Alone in the Crowd
3.   **My Presence is Essential**
3.1.   My Well-being is Central
3.2.   Motherhood: A Two-Way Guilt
3.3.   Pressure to Create a New Home
4.   **Making Sense of Who I am and Who I want to Be**
4.1.   Who Am I in this New World?
4.2.   Making Sense of my Presence
4.3.   The Need for Personal Success

Figure 1: Brief Outline of Master Themes

The master themes were organized around the different processes of meaning making that participants engaged in, namely their attempts at understanding what it meant to be a WOD across diplomatic assignments. Accordingly, it appeared that WODs acknowledged the (1) need for a strong base in their marriage, in order to (2) allow themselves to lose part of their identity. This first thread allowed them to (3) understand the importance of their presence in these diplomatic assignments and eventually (4) make sense of who they are and who they want to be.

The analysis uses data in the form of direct quotes from the transcribed interview. In order for the participants' identities to stay protected, their names and any identifying information have been changed. These changes mainly include a pseudonymous given name, and countries and cities where WODs and their families have been posted. The latter have been changed following a specific coding system; for example, if the participant lived in Rio de Janeiro, the information has been altered as [Important South American City].

When quoting from the transcript, the pseudonym, page number, and line numbers are mentioned in parenthesis after the quote. The quotes were left entirely unedited, and were presented with participants' original expressions and language, including syntax and grammatical errors, in order to stay as close as possible to their stories. Pauses and silences are indicated in the text by the use of a double full stop (..), while the use of italic text within parentheses is used to describe non-verbal reactions. The use of bold text is utilized for words that were stressed by the participant. In a few cases, the use of brackets without text indicates that a part of the text has been omitted for style or comprehensibility.

One factor that runs through the participants' narratives is the importance of culture and context in understanding how they made sense of their experiences. However, due to the differences in cultures represented in the sample, I felt that emphasizing culture and context at a thematic level would risk losing the richness of experiences that were common among WODs. Therefore, I have woven culture and context into the analysis at each point where I felt it would inform the reader of the background to the experiences being described.

3.1   Master Theme 1 – Power of Marriage

This master theme illustrates the way all eight WODs under study view the importance of marriage as the strongest base in diplomatic assignments. Each participant described her marriage as the main vessel to the quality of diplomatic assignments and how this factor was fundamental to their experience. The need to be part of a team with their husbands was a direct link to their involvement in assignments and acceptance of their new lives.

3.1.1   Love

Most participants described "Love" as being the central element of their marriages and regarded it as the initial reason for agreeing to accompany their husbands. As most of them met in professional environments, they all described needing to love unconditionally in order to leave the lives they had initially construed and embark on this new journey.

Amy, for example, described meeting her husband, falling deeply in love with him, and needing to be with him at any cost:

It was love at first sight. (Amy, p. 10, l. 139)

I was anxious and nervous, but I mean I loved him so much that I wanted to be with him at any price. I am telling you, the love is the most important thing to be able to go through all this. (Amy, p. 25, l. 356-358)

Amy referred to her love for her husband as starting from the first moment they met. Her vivid recollection of feeling anxious and nervous about this new life indicated that she could not have moved away from her home if it was not for the genuine love she had for her husband. Her use of the locution "I am telling you" seemed to suggest that she is absolutely convinced of what the power of love can do to people, and how "love" was the most important element that allowed her to "go through all this." It is as if she painted an image of herself finding the strength to embark on this life through the need of being with him "at any price."

> But I realize that we need the will and the love in order to do it. The will and the love, but I think the love is more important because when there is love, the will comes. (Lina, 20, l. 281-283)

Lina described her sense of acceptance and entry into this world as a result of the "will and love" she had. Her language and repetition of "the will and the love" suggested that her transition was only possible because of these two components. She then seemed to acknowledge that will and love were not two independent components, but mutually causative. She identified will as the result of the love she felt for her husband, and understood that this will was needed in order to become part of diplomatic assignments.

> Love is important because it keeps you together, it keeps the couple strong, the couple should be strong to go through all the changes, you know. It's not easy. (Lina, p. 36, l. 519-521)

Lina's acknowledgment of love as essential seemed further compounded in her belief that it was what kept her marriage strong. Her experience of going "through all the changes" was one that was "not easy," but was possible because they were "strong." Similarly, her marriage's strength was also the result of the love they had and shared.

> It makes you see the other differently and makes you cope and makes you make a lot of effort. So already a marriage is not easy, but abroad it's even worse, and so you need to really love the person to do all these efforts. (Caline, p. 17, l. 246-248)

Likewise, Caline described a marriage abroad as very difficult and needing great effort. Although from her language it seemed that she encountered many difficulties, the love she had for her husband allowed her to keep going and make the necessary efforts to make her marriage work. It seemed that love was the element that prevented her from quitting.

These experiences of deep and mutual love seemed to have helped WODs' transitions, suggesting that without love, their experiences would have been different and qualitatively worse. These feelings engendered a sense of belonging in a couple and being part of a team, in which both members played a key role in each other's life. This is explored further in the next subtheme.

3.1.2   Togetherness

This sub-theme explores how WODs perceived their roles in diplomatic assignments. It shows the understanding of WODs' capacity for being part of the assignment, while being in the background, as expressed by Louise:

> You know my role was not official, or like people couldn't see exactly my input in his work, but behind the door, we were working together (Louise, 27, l. 349-350)

It appears that the very experience of working with her husband "behind the door" influenced her sense of belonging in a team. Although these assignments were officially for the diplomats, the inclusion of the wife in the official process seemed to have increased Louise's sense of usefulness and understanding her purpose, allowing her to find her a place both in the assignment and in her marriage. Louise did not seem preoccupied by others seeing her "input in his work," which emphasized her need to be a team player with him. She also seemed to link the unofficiality of her role to others' ability of seeing what she was doing, suggesting that only their perception could have officialized it.

Similarly, Sarah explained how her role was quite important, although foreseen as unofficial.

> I help him quite a lot, unofficially of course, like gathering information, I read his speeches, I sometimes write like, uh, drafts…for his comments…for his reports before he sends them to the ministry (Sarah, p. 2, l. 30-31)

Sarah's "of course" suggested that she recognized her limited role and felt no need to refute it. Her enumeration, however, emphasized her awareness of her role and the different ways in which she helped her husband in official duties. On the other hand, this togetherness was highlighted by her husband's acceptance and openness to her help, accentuating their team work.

> When he has some things to share from an economical point of view, he knows and says 'what do you think of this report?' The secretary of the embassy wrote it but what's **your** comment? and I also have a comment that he approves (Marta, p. 23, l. 258-263)

Sarah and Marta had experiences of helping their husbands with their official work, while having their intellectual abilities acknowledged by them. Both their statements suggested that their husbands relied upon their wives' opinions in their assignments, rather than excluding them from their work. Marta showed how her husband's request was one that is intentional, as he valued her unique opinion.

Likewise, Lina remembered:

> We always consult with each other. We brainstorm together and discuss things together about his work. (Lina, p. 17, l. 247-248)

Lina related her experience of working in a different capacity with her husband. Her sense of togetherness was highlighted by her repetition of the word "we" and "together." It was however contrasted with her inference of "his work," reminding herself that she was only part of his world. In a way, she showed that her input was not only valued but also crucial to the practical side of diplomatic assignments.

> We used to plan everything, even conversation. Like we would say ok this conversation let's not open it. Let's focus on that instead. We used to do that my husband and I. (Lina, p. 25, l. 582-584)

Lina later gave an example of another instance when she and her husband engaged in teamwork. Again, her repetition of the pronoun "we" emphasized her willingness to be part of her husband's work, and the specificity of her example implied her high level of understanding of the diplomatic world. In fact, by planning social conversations, Lina experienced herself as part of the micro-activities that took place, increasing her sense of usefulness.

> I became useful for him because I would share tips or information that I learned about the country or the people with him. Like you know they told me this and look how they act (Marta, p. 22, l. 252-254)

Marta described her sense of usefulness by being an ally to her husband. She shared "tips or information" to which he did not have access, suggesting that she had a different type of insight that could have potentially helped him. Marta also recognized her role as the missing piece of the puzzle:

> I wouldn't say that it was also crucial information, but more information that was complimentary. Like if my husband had a meeting with someone I would say I played bridge with his wife and they really enjoy this or that. I had information that maybe helped how do you say smooth a meeting or make the other person more comfortable with my husband (Marta, p. 23, l. 258-262)

However, as Marta further elaborated her role, she seemed to not think of it as "crucial," but rather as a "smooth[er]" to the process. Her experience suggested a lower level of involvement, as opposed to Lina who experienced higher levels of involvement.

This sub-theme suggested different varieties of involvement, all appearing to play a crucial role in the WODs' senses of purpose. Their appreciation for togetherness seemed to help WOD connect further with their husbands and experience themselves as key team players in these assignments. Given their sense of togetherness, both husband and wife are expected to play important roles in each other's lives and provide the right environment and support to help the other flourish as the person they want to be. The importance of this support is further developed in the final sub-theme.

3.1.3   Emotional Support

For most participants, husbands' support and understanding was an important element to which they referred to on many occasions throughout their interviews. It often seemed as though the support they received allowed them to stay congruent with themselves.

Some WODs received help from their husbands while experiencing their transitions, as Elan described.

> But he knew I was like that, so every time we had to host a dinner, he would ask how much would it be if we catered the food, so this amount will go to me instead since I was doing everything. And I think it's also the type of person I am because I didn't want to just ask for the money itself, I wanted to feel like I worked for it. That was tough. (Elan, p. 37, l. 542-546)

Elan explained that one of the biggest challenges she faced when she embarked on this new journey was becoming financially dependent on her husband. As she highlighted her concern, she experienced her husband as an understanding man who "knew [she] was like that" and created a compensation system for her efforts. Elan seemed to feel supported by him as he showed cooperativeness and appreciation for her efforts. Most importantly, it did not seem that Elan was asked to change, as she was able to stay true to herself while finding creative ways with her husband to do so. She experienced this need to feel worthy as "tough," but was alleviated by her husband's support.

> He understands what I need. If he didn't I wouldn't have been able to continue all of this. (Marta, p. 18, l. 200-201)

This quote went to the very heart of Marta's experience of being a WOD. It showed how her husband's support was the main element that allowed her to continue this journey with him. His dedication to understand what she needed at this time made her feel heard and understood in their marriage.

> I think my husband met me half way. I know he made a lot of efforts to understand me. He would understand that sometimes I was too tired with the kids and that I did not want to go out. Or you know he would say let's invite some people instead. (Caline, p. 14, l. 199-202)

In line with Marta and Elan, Caline explained how being heard and taken into consideration helped her cope with her presence in diplomatic assignments. Meeting her husband "half way" implied the balance and equal partnership they experienced in their marriage. Caline's appreciation for her husband's efforts suggested that perhaps it was not something she truly expected from him, but was receiving nevertheless. His ability to create new alternatives that would better suit Caline showed the usefulness of the support system he put in place for her.

This master theme explored the power that marriage holds in participants' experiences of being in diplomatic assignments, by looking at the sub-themes of "love," "togetherness," and "mental support." There was a rich harmony in the accounts within these sub-themes, suggesting that being in a healthy marriage was an important aspect of WODs' experiences during diplomatic assignments. In all accounts, the WODs interviewed projected the image that they were not following their husbands on postings, but rather accompanying them, suggesting greater respect and value for their role.

3.2   Master Theme 2 – Loss of Self

In this master theme, WODs reflected on their experiences as individuals. The participants described diplomatic assignments and the effect it had on their senses of self. They also expressed how this experience made them lose some aspect of themselves, as they rapidly realized that had no control or place to share their personal opinions and worries.

This section first looks at (1) how these diplomatic assignments were experienced as "not about them," and (2) how their sense of control disappeared as many factors depended on external bodies. It then (3) deals with WODs' worries about wasted intellectual potential and (4) how they sometimes found themselves feeling alone and isolated.

3.2.1   This is Not About Me

The effect of becoming a WOD was first experienced by the realization that they were embarking on a journey that was not about them. Therefore, the WODs needed to adjust to the demands of these assignments, which led them to lose a part of themselves in the process.

> The only thing that I have to accept strongly although I don't approve is that, although you are a diplomatic spouse, you cannot say what you feel, because you are not you. [ ] In my case, I am representing my country, so my husband said 'remember, it's not

about you anymore, it's about your country now. You are your country. So be careful what you say'... It was so difficult for me to understand this. (Elan, p. 26, l. 376-382)

It appeared that the very experience of finding out that she was a symbol and a representation of something bigger led Elan to conclude that she was not able to embrace herself completely and fully. The oxymoronic concept that "you are not you" brought much confusion into understanding this new identity that she needed to adopt in the eye of the public. She further explained the impact of not understanding this shift:

So many times my husband and I would argue after a dinner or something. And he would be like, 'why did you say that? You came across as rude! You can't always be yourself, you are [home country], not Elan.' (Elan, p. 27, l. 392-395)

Elan described not conforming to the norms and holding on to her own sense of self, leading her to experience conflicts with her husband. On the other hand, her husband understood what diplomatic assignments entailed and how they transformed a person into a symbol. Although Elan was reporting his words, she remembered being told that being herself "came across as rude" and that some elements of her personality were not allowed. These conditions suggested that Elan's understanding of representing a country translated into losing aspects of herself.

But, eh, sometimes you get into trouble if you don't control yourself. So it's like a responsibility to not be yourself. It's a pressure, but you know it's for political reasons and also other things, like you cannot comment on, eh, things you don't like to hear. It's like you can't share your opinion, or if you want to, if you have to think 10 times before you speak...it's exhausting. Because at the end of the day, you just want to be yourself. You want to be able to say whatever comes to your mind and have no boundaries; you just want to be free. (Lina, p. 15, l. 209-216)

Lina talked about needing to control herself and to "think 10 times" before she spoke in order to avoid being in "trouble." Having to control elements of her personality was an exhausting pressure that she needed to apply every time she was in presence of others. Her use of the words "boundaries" and "free" suggested that she may have felt imprisoned in the body of a person that she did not recognize, as she had a "responsibility to not be [her]self." Lina asserted that she could not share her personal opinions for political reasons, as her expressed opinions represented her country, not her. Likewise, Caline described her experience of feeling detached:

> Very impersonal. I gain nothing. I go in a certain mind set where I know that I just need to say this sentence like 'congratulations for your independence day', and that's it. Nothing more nothing less. It's impersonal because my presence is irrelevant for the bigger picture. But that's for the official part; you know you have to be there but it does not need to be **you you**, just the wife of the [home country] diplomat. (Caline, 20, l. 281-283)

Caline referred to her experience of being a symbol as impersonal and insignificant. She showed awareness at the irrelevance of her presence and understood that her role in the capacity of a WOD was solely a form of display. She referred to the need of actively putting herself in "a certain mind set," where the impact of her presence was rectified and adjusted to the reality of her role as a WOD. Caline's verbal and non-verbal communication at the time suggested that she voluntarily disconnected from these official duties, as she understood that her presence there had nothing to do with the person she was. She reflected on the way being a WOD had led her to feel that her sense of self had been changed, as the focus shifted from her to the job itself.

Sarah experiences a similar feeling of having to lose a part of herself in order to simply be a WOD.

I'm representing something. I am not myself. I make this huge difference. I am myself now, like when I talk to my good friends, but in these dinners, cocktails, I am not myself. I am representing a person. I don't know what I am exactly but I know it's not me. (Marta, p. 40, l. 454-456)

Marta referred to herself as being a symbol, rather than her true self. She suggested not being able to know exactly who she was but seemed to be certain that she was not herself in specific situations. Also, Marta appeared to know exactly in what moments her true self disappeared, suggesting that it was like a mask she put on and off when the situation felt appropriate.

She told him one thing 'for the ministry you are you, you are not a family' because he told her 'my wife, my kids, school, blabla, think about us, how can you do that?'. She told him 'you are you, nobody is going to think that you are married and have a family.' (Amy, p. 29, l. 413-416)

Amy described feeling disregarded by the ministry of foreign affairs. She reported hearing the secretary of the ministry explain to her husband that for the ministry, her husband was considered alone, and she and her children were never taken into the equation, which accentuated Amy's invisibility to them. Amy's syntax suggested that she was feeling angry for being left out and not cared for, given that it was assumed that she was supposed to follow her husband and not argue any decisions taken by the ministry.

While this sub-theme illustrated how WODs experienced diplomatic assignments as constricted and unimportant, the next sub-theme deals with their loss of sense of control in assignments.

3.2.2. Loss of Agency

All participants experienced a transition of control over their lives as they accompanied their husbands in diplomatic postings. The felt that their senses of agency and autonomy were taken away from them, handing all forms of self-control to other entities, such as their national foreign services.

One of the aspects of this loss of control is financial. Some participants described their first proof of loss of agency by their financial dependency on their husband. This dependency played an important role in their lives as it represented the shift from being independent working women to being WODs. For example, Elan described her experience of being financially dependent on her husband, where the emphasis was put on her previous life.

> Not having an income that was tough, you know, to depend on your husband. I have **never never never** depended on someone in my adult life when it came to my needs; I worked on holidays, worked on scholarships. (Elan, p. 36, l. 535-537)

Elan's vivid recollection of never having to depend financially on someone in her adult life showed how important her dependency was for her. The repetition of the word "never" illustrated how financial independence was crucially significant for her and the use of examples on how she earned money suggested a sense of personal accomplishment. The use of the word "tough" seemed to mark this transition as one of the main obstacles she faced as a WOD.

> But still it was part of my personality. Tough to change like that and 'gosh, now I have to ask **him** for money,' uh (shaking head) like that was really tough thing. (Elan, p. 37, l. 540-541)

Elan's sense of acceptance seemed to be one that came with great difficulties. The use of the words "tough," and "gosh," and her non-verbal communication, suggested that her financial dependency was not desired but imposed upon her.

Similarly, Louise described living with money that was "his":

I don't have a salary so we really live with **his** money. It was very weird because my whole life I worked and made my own money, and to then go and ask him for things...euh...I remember times where I didn't...hmmm... didn't' even know how to ask for it (Louise, p. 57, l. 766-771)

Louise seemed to be repulsed by the feeling of asking for money as she recalled a life where she had her "own money." Her pauses and hesitations suggested a difficulty to acknowledge that her financial dependency was real, and that her life had somewhat changed.

Along with being financially dependent, becoming a WOD is a transition that many experienced as difficult given the uncertainty of their future.

That's when I realized that my life was going to change. (Nervous laughing), I did not know anything about the diplomatic life. I knew things were going to be different but I did not know how. (Ava, p. 5, l. 59-62)

Ava recalls the first moment she was told that she would be assisting her husband on their first diplomatic assignment. She appeared feeling afraid of stepping into an unknown world, as she was unable to know what to expect. Her fear was emphasized by her nervous laughter, suggesting that the uncertainty made her feel worried. This discomfort in uncertainty is further being experienced when moving to a new country:

The thing is that we have no control to where they send us. We can't even request anything and that makes me **sooooo** nervous...this uncertainty. (Ava, p. 46, l. 678-680)

Ava's lack of control on the situation was experienced through the process of moving to a new country. Her prolonged "so" draws attention to how difficult it was to live with such uncertainty. Her need to make requests implied that Ava may have had specific reasons why she would have preferred to go to a certain country, rather than leaving it up to random assignment.

Elan also experienced this sense of uncertainty, feeling that she was living in an environment that was not hers:

> The thing is that husbands are safe because when they meet among each other, the topics discussed are quite formal like economics and politics and topics that are work related so no extra effort. But when it comes to **us**, it can be anything and everything. (Elan, p. 17, l. 241-244)

Elan expressed a sense of separation between her experience as the WOD and the experience of her husband as the diplomat. This element of "us-versus-them" resonated throughout Elan's description of how it felt to be on the other side of the same world. The use of the word "safe" suggested that perhaps Elan did not feel as safe and protected in her part of the world. Her reference to "anything and everything" echoes a real lack of certainty and security of what her role is supposed to be.

Other WODs, such as Lina, experienced satisfaction in the countries they had been assigned to, while acknowledging that these were purely based on luck:

> I went to [important North American city] and [North American Capital], and [Mediterranean European Country]. But what if I went to like [Asian under-developed country] and was stuck there, or to [Northern European Country] or whatever. It's not easy because a lot of luck comes to play. And I was lucky. (Lina, p. 38, l. 527-531)

Lina considered the location of her diplomatic assignments to be an important element of her quality of life. She expressed awareness of the potential consequences of being somewhere else, leading her to feel a certain sense of gratitude. However, the realization that her life depended on a variable that was out of her control created a sense of powerlessness, leading her to experience feelings of anxiety.

> There was a lot of uncertainty. And that uncertainty killed me, even though I am very flexible. (Caline, p. 29, l. 425-426)

Caline's experience of uncertainty was "kill[ing] her," suggesting that it affected her quality of life. She defined herself as a "very flexible" person, signifying that diplomatic assignments were abnormally uncertain, as nothing was in her control.

Additionally, Elan gave an example of the worries she experienced as a result of her lack of agency.

> I mean like one of my worries is the fact that I do not have a permanent doctor that knows my health and me. So every time I move, I have to change doctors and some will advise you based on the country you are in, like diets, medicines, things like that. And like everything changes, the weather and you know it is our responsibility to not neglect it but it is beyond our control (Elan, p 45, l. 665-669)

Elan's worry about not having a stable medical doctor who knew her complete medical history had been one of her main sources of stress, given her need for permanency. Having to change physicians every couple of years suggested a need to start over every time, a process that can be tiring and overwhelming. Moreover, she emphasized multiple factors beyond her control that affected her physical and mental health, while acknowledging the importance of not neglecting them.

Louise explained this lack of control further:

> You are most of the time not in control of the situation…as a trailing wife, most things are out of control. The countries you go to, how you dress, what you say, the dinners, the food, you don't have a lot of space to make big decisions and you have to be okay with that. (Louise, p. 46, l. 654-657)

This quote went to the very heart of how Louise experienced diplomatic assignments. First, she referred to herself as a "trailing wife," suggesting that she perceived herself as solely following her husband in diplomatic assignments, although this was the terminology used when Louise's husband was a diplomat. Second, her life seemed to be dictated by her diplomatic duties and roles, implying that there was little space for her to experience her true self. Louise appeared, however, to have made sense of the challenges that diplomatic assignments convey, and understood that the only way to go through them was by accepting them. Her initiative in accepting and not refuting these "out of control" scenarios allowed Louise to accept a loss of self, at least to a certain extent.

This loss of agency was also experienced by the limitations WODs experienced with regard to their places of domicile.

> As ambassadors we are not allowed to choose our house, we live in the house that is given to us…with the same furniture and all. (Sarah, p. 28, l. 318-320)

Choosing one's house was an element that many people needed in order to feel at home when moving countries, as they could personalize it. Given that the ministry of foreign affairs assigned the same house with the same furniture to every diplomat and his family, Sarah's sense of uniqueness was affected. Moreover, her use of the phrase "not allowed" illustrated the limited amount of control she had over their choice of domicile.

> Every time you want to buy like a plate, you have to ask permission from [home country]. Also like if you want to throw something, you put them in the bag and have to send them to [home country]. (Amy, p. 15, l. 214-217)

Amy gives an example of how she felt limited in diplomatic assignments. She explained not having enough freedom as she needed to "ask permission" to take make decisions. Her choice of example showed the extent to which her loss of agency was affected: Amy described her lack of control by explaining how throwing out something that was no longer of use required permission from her home country. This emphasized her inability to take initiative without permission, suggesting another dimension of dependency and loss of autonomy.

> The hardest thing was not being able to buy what you wanted. Asking for permission was unimaginable at first, but then you have no choice but to get used to it. (Caline, p.39, l. 566-568)

As Amy and Caline represent the same country, Caline also described her lack of freedom as the "hardest thing." Her use of the word "unimaginable" highlighted how she first perceived the irrationality of this rule. Caline, however, came to terms with it as she recognized the absence of choice and the extent of her powerlessness.

> We lived in the consulate, and you sleep there but it's not your stuff! The bed is not yours, the bathroom is not yours, the kitchen is not yours. Nothing was yours! I mean how stupid is that?! (Caline, p. 40, l. 573-576)

Although Caline seemed at times to have accepted the situation as it was, she later expressed anger. Her exclamation at the end of the first sentence denoted fury. Her attempt to explain her sense of rootlessness was accentuated by the enumeration of the rooms in the house, and the repetition of the locution "is not yours." While affirming that "nothing was [hers]," Caline seemed to experience insecurity, given her lack of belongings. Ownership seemed to hold a significant meaning for her and experiencing her house as not her own appears to have affected her ability to form a basic attachment to it. Her rhetorical question and use of the word "stupid" clearly indicated her anger, discomfort, and confusion about the situation.

The most difficult thing was for my husband and I to understand that everything that we had belonged to the job and not to us. Like one minute you have a team that comes and picks you up from the airport with flags on your car, and the other minute you are left alone, figuring out how to take the tube and commute your way in [Major European City]. (Louise, p. 48, l. 732-735)

Here, Louise portrayed a sense of awareness that came once her husband had retired. She expressed realizing that the material items they used and every service offered to them "belonged to the job" and not to them, suggesting a lack of sense of ownership.

On the other hand, Elan's sense of dependency also resulted from her inability to commit to any professional opportunities given her attachment to her husband's postings.

My university offered me to do my masters because there was a need for special need children and pay for it but that would mean that I would be bonded to them for five years and I knew that we needed to leave for his first posting, so I had to turn it down. (Elan, p. 5, l. 72-76)

Elan described needing to leave with her husband at the expense of her own academic and professional growth. This suggested another level of dependency, where her academic and professional growth could have only happened when diplomatic postings aligned with her professional opportunities.

This sub-theme has illustrated how WODs experienced the transition between a life in which they had a sense of control and autonomy to a new life in which they ceded control to someone else's career and depended on luck. In the next sub-theme, we will explore how diplomatic assignments affects WODs' intellectual potential.

3.2.3   Wasted Intellectual Potential

As mentioned, most WODs met their husbands in professional settings, and their intellectual and professional identities played a role in their self-concept prior to diplomatic postings. Hence, becoming a WOD unavoidably affected their views of their intellectual potential, as their identity felt threatened by the absence of their own professional identity.

For some, this experience was mainly driven by regrets and loss of personal potential, while others compared their intellectual demands to their husbands'. Elan spent time describing what she could have been if she had stayed in her home country. She appeared many times to have believed that she wasted intellectual potential applicable to different areas in her life. At times, being a WOD seemed to have held some regrets for her:

> *(Looking down)* Well the biggest disappointment was not being able to do my masters. (Elan, p. 38, l. 558)

Several times during the interview, Elan expressed, both verbally and non-verbally, a disappointment in herself for not having the chance to pursue her studies. She explained that as a result of becoming a WOD, her academic growth had to stop, leading her and others to feel that she had wasted an opportunity:

> Um, well the thing is that my family really thought I would end up being somebody very successful in her job and become somebody important in which ever field because I really had potential. So for them, for me to do this was like 'Oh my God, what is she doing with her life? It is such a waste.' (Elan, p. 18, l. 255-258)

Elan's experience of being a WOD initially started with remorse and guilt. Her family's perception seemed to be one that she carried most heavily. In thinking "Oh my God, what is she doing with her life? It is such a waste," observers seemed to have undervalued Elan's identity and role as a WOD. Being seen as a waste of potential appeared to be a belief that Elan understood and to some extent agreed with, as she was conscious that she "really had potential" in an academic field.

Additionally, Sarah reflected on her past year in her current assignment and said:

> I sometimes think about that myself as well. And where did I, what did I do during the last year? Uh, what did I do that was intellectually challenging or meaningful? (Sarah, p. 37, l. 495-497)

Sarah appeared to question her previous year's accomplishments. Her self-reflection suggested that it was as if the past year had not been meaningful enough given her lack of intellectual challenges.

Marta described similar views the first time her husband advised her to engage in social activities during their first posting:

> When I finished my paper after 1 year, I became very upset because I did not have anything else to do other than reading the newspaper. So my husband told me 'why don't you do like the other wives do, and go learn a new activity like mahjong or bridge?' I was so angry with him for telling me that because I had just finished writing a very important article that was going to be published in one of the biggest economics journal and for him to tell me that, it felt like an insult. (Marta, p. 19-20, l. 218-223)

Marta asserted here the unsettling nature of her experience. She hinted at a sense of disappointment towards her husband, who advised her to become "like the other wives." Marta's quote suggested that she had a personal opinion of WODs and felt that her professional accomplishments could not be replaced by parlor games. Her anger was justified by her self-image and ideal self being insulted, as she felt that she had gone from being a highly regarded professional to a bored WOD.

This experience of "me versus them" was also experienced by Ava, who compared her intellectual expectations to her husband's.

> He had to mingle with the other men and I had to mingle with the other wives. He had to talk politics and I would talk about irrelevant things like recipes and curtains (laughs), oh my God, such irrelevant topics. (Ava, p. 20, l. 285-287)

For Ava, being a WOD required her to mingle and socialize with other WODs. The structure and tone of her quote suggested a real sense of separation between herself and husband. She suggested that her husband was expected to talk about serious and meaningful topics, while she was asked to talk about "irrelevant" topics that emphasized her role as a WOD. Her laugh and exclamation of "oh my God" reflected the lack of seriousness she experienced within herself and a certain recognition that her intellectual potential was being wasted on banal topics.

Louise shared similar views on the intellectual deterioration she was experiencing.

> We are not allowed to work, because we are made to be social and go to tea parties, which I had to do, but it wasn't me. (Louise, p. 37, l. 542-543)

Louise poignantly explained that her intellectual potential was not being challenged enough because she was not allowed to work. Her use of the expression "we are made to" referred to others' expectations of her role in diplomatic assignments, and how the context around her was molded in a way that did not give her the agency to do as she wished.

> I remember once when we were in [important North American city], I told my husband, I feel like I'm regressing, and that my mind is shrinking, you know. I am feeling that I am stupid, that I am going backwards. (Caline, p. 13, l. 185-188)

Here, Caline draws a picture of how it felt for her to be the WOD on their first assignment. Her analogy of her mind "shrinking" made her feel "stupid and going backwards," suggesting that she did not recognize herself anymore.

> I was afraid of being empty…intellectually empty. (Marta, p. 5, l. 55)

Marta reflected on her fear of being intellectually empty, suggesting that her intellectual abilities and professional role were important elements that defined her identity but lost in her life as a WOD.

This sub-theme focused on one of the facets that led WOD to feel a loss of self. Their inability to express and experience their intellectual selves fully had affected their quality of life and distorted the lens through which they perceived themselves. In this final sub-theme, WODs explored how they felt about losing a part of themselves as they were embarking on a very lonely journey.

3.2.4   Alone in the Crowd

Most participants explained that being on diplomatic assignments felt like living an isolated life, as they were alone most of the time. Some WODs referred to losing parts of their identities, as they were not being able to find a place in these assignments.

Ava described diplomatic assignments as a place where she felt lonely:

> The reality is loneliness. You are at home alone. You don't have family. You are alone. (Ava, p. 37, l. 534)

Ava's sense of loneliness was emphasized by the repetition of the word "alone." Her paralinguistic choice and tone conveyed real sadness in the awareness that it was a lonely world for her. Her use of the word "reality" suggested that others' perceptions of diplomatic assignments was different from the reality.

Caline provided an explanation for why she felt lonely during diplomatic assignments:

> There's not enough time to develop profound friendships. Maybe in your community, but it stays very superficial. You don't get to know someone very deeply in 2-3 years, so most of the time you feel alone. (Caline, p. 37, l. 541-544)

Caline made sense of why it was difficult to build friendships and belong to an unconditional and genuine social group. Her sense of belonging seemed superficial and insufficient.

> Until you build your own environment with people who share the same concepts, you feel quite alone. This was a bit hard. (Sarah, p. 12, l. 136-137)

Sarah suggested that not having a sense of belonging made it harder to be on diplomatic assignments. It seemed to her that looking for others who shared similar "concepts" was an important element that prevented her from feeling alone.

Although this process may have been difficult given the short length of their stays, Elan explained the importance of having a good relationship within one's self, as diplomatic assignments are a solitary process:

> You must learn to enjoy yourself because it gets lonely and it gets difficult, and you need to have a good relationship with yourself to be able to handle these moments. (Elan, p. 41, l. 652-653)

Elan highlighted the importance of being congruent and enjoying her own presence because diplomatic assignments were difficult. She linked loneliness with difficulty, suggesting that her lack of belonging affected the quality of her life in diplomatic assignments.

In this sub-theme, WODs' accounts of loneliness suggested that a sense of belonging was important in order to experience themselves fully while accompanying their husbands on diplomatic assignments.

This master theme focused on the way WODs experienced themselves while on assignments. Their possible loss of self was one of the main determinants of the quality of the lives they lived and the way they felt about their identities. The next master theme will explore the roles they occupied in these assignments, and how they experience their presence as central.

3.3   Master Theme 3 – My Presence is Essential

Many participants reflected on the roles they occupied when accompanying their husbands, first by the person they decided to be in these assignments, and second by the burden they had to carry. In the first sub-theme, "My Attitude is Central," WODs described how their attitudes and perceptions of diplomatic assignments affected the experience of diplomatic postings for husbands and children. The second sub-theme, "Motherhood: A Two-Way Guilt" focused on both the effect of being a mother during diplomatic assignments and the guilt that could be associated with it. In the last sub-theme, "Pressure to Create a New Home," WODs reflected on the duty they had towards their families to create a new home during every diplomatic assignment.

3.3.1   My Well-Being is Central

Most WODs referred to their well-being as an important element in the quality of the assignment. They explained how their attitudes and perceptions with regard to diplomatic assignments affected their well-being and explained that it was how they decided to embrace the experience that helped their husbands succeed. As Caline explained:

> My husband says 'you're the balance.' And I realize that I am not allowed to think a lot or to feel anything. Because if I don't do well or don't feel well, the family will collapse. Like even now, I think he is very stressed whenever he feels that I am stressed. (Caline, p. 32, l. 502-504)

Caline described how she experienced her role in her family as a pillar that supported the whole. She seemed not to allow herself the luxury of thinking and feeling, suggesting that she would numb her sentiments in order to preserve balance in the family. Caline felt the pressure of being the centrality of her family as any given imbalance in herself could have resulted in its destruction.

> You know, holding it all together for the sake of the children and my husband…that was difficult. (Louise, p. 37, l. 502-503)

Louise expressed similar feelings in regards to her role in the family. She painted a picture of needing to hold "it all together," suggesting that if she had not done so, major consequences could have followed.

Lina talked at length about how she felt about the importance of WODs in assignments. She gave examples of times when she witnessed the effect of an unhappy WOD:

> You know, if the woman does not understand and is not engaged with the job, then it's a huge headache. I remember a colleague of us [sic] was a very good diplomat but his wife did not like any of it. So she kept on nagging, nagging, nagging because she wasn't happy and he had to resign from this posting. He took on a different job in their country. (Lina, p. 18, l. 272-276)

Lina attempted to prove the importance of the WOD's well-being. She acknowledged that assignments do not only depend on diplomats, but that spouses' satisfaction was equally crucial. Lina seemed to refer to the unhappy WOD she knew as someone who did not understand the job and hence disengaged from it, suggesting that diplomatic postings depended on these elements. She further explained how these dynamics can be affected while on diplomatic duties.

> One of the most important factor is the wife's well-being. Because if the wife is not happy, the children are not happy, and the dynamics are affected. (Lina, p. 19, l. 277-278)

Lina identified another consequence of being an unhappy WOD, while suggesting that her well-being was at the center of her family's. She referred to dynamics being affected, suggesting that her well-being should be taken into consideration and valued by others. Lina continued by explaining how and why a WOD should try to have a good attitude towards these assignments:

> It's not easy. You have to like the lifestyle and on top of it, you have to accept that you keep changing: habits, friends, homes. If you are not crazy about this kind of life, it's not an easy life. (Lina, p. 46, l. 521-525)

When asked about what advice Lina would give future WODs, she first acknowledged that adopting a positive attitude was difficult. She then explained how the most important element was one's ability to "like the lifestyle." Lina seemed to be aware that constant change was the most difficult factor in diplomatic assignments and that WODs needed to be able to accept and embrace it.

Both Caline and Louise explained how adaptability had been of high importance when accompanying their husbands on assignments:

> I think I have a good quality, which is adaptation. I am a Gemini (laughs). So I get adapted very easily (Caline, p. 3, l. 31-32)

I mean my own flexibility really helped. I am very adaptable. I'm sure it's a lot of my character, too. (Louise, p. 14, l. 202-203)

Both appeared to praise themselves for having this positive quality. They seemed to refer to their ability to adapt to change as a way of connecting and engaging further in diplomatic assignments.

So yeah, like, I used to go for every assignment with him with an open mind and with an idea that we have to succeed. And this is why we were a team. (Ava, p. 18, l. 265-267)

Ava described her attitude at the beginning of each assignment as her way of engaging with and embracing them. She referred to her ability to start each with an "open mind," leading her to connect further with her husband and express her closeness to him.

I was ready to learn and to do what was best for him and to make him look good. (Amy, p. 13, l. 198-199)

Amy referred to her willingness to be there for her husband by learning the different things she needed to do as a WOD. Her attitude seemed to be of great importance as she portrayed great motivation to "make him look good" and be the best version of herself, for him.

This sub-theme has illustrated how a WOD's attitude and mindset were perceived as important elements in the well-being of the family and the quality of diplomatic assignments. The next sub-theme deals with the role participants had as mothers and its effect on their well-being.

3.3.2   Motherhood: A Two-Way Guilt

All participants who have children talked at length about their role as mothers in diplomatic assignments. For them, being a mother was the biggest challenge they faced while on these postings, as they experienced great difficulties in balancing their roles as WODs and mothers. Most of them admitted to never being able to make the right decision, as they always felt like they were caught up in a dilemma.

> It's complicated to be a mother and a spouse. So, you have one foot here, and one other foot there. So, in some assignments with my husband, especially the one in [Major Middle Eastern City], especially this one, I had to be here and there…(pause)…It's not easy to have…the most, maybe, the most difficult part is to have children abroad. (Ava, p. 5-6, l. 69-82)

Ava described the two main roles she occupied on postings as conflicting. She portrayed an image of being caught up between two places that needed her attention. While Ava referred to one assignment specifically where her presence was particularly more important, she took a long pause. During this moment of silence, Ava looked down and seemed to have been carried away by her thoughts, suggesting that she had recalled a sad memory. She confirmed her sadness by explaining that the most difficult challenge she experienced during diplomatic assignments was to be a mother.

Similarly, Amy explained her difficulty in juggling between her roles:

> If you have this kind of double life, it's difficult because you are always in the wrong place, you have the bad conscience if you are too much with your husband then you are not enough with your kids. If you are with your kids, you are not supporting your husband enough. You are not hosting this and this event, you are not going to this and this dinner invitation. (Amy, p. 33, l. 438-443)

Amy's reference to having a double life suggested that she experienced herself as two different people. Her reality was one of constantly having a "bad conscience," signifying that whatever decision she took, she would still be neglecting another area. Amy's inability to please both parties appeared to create a sentiment of guilt, which Lina talked about in her experience of two-way guilt:

> Guilt, guilt, guilt always guilt. If you go to a dinner and you know they are at home watching TV, you feel guilty because you left them. Especially when you just arrive in a new post, because when you arrive there you want to succeed and to succeed you have to be out there. (Lina, p. 22, l. 314-317)

Lina's repetition of the word guilt highlighted the pain she experienced from being both a WOD and a mother. She attempted at explaining her guilt by giving an example of times she felt this guilt vividly. Lina referred to the beginning of diplomatic assignments as an important time for her husband, given the importance of succeeding. However, she seemed to also be aware that the beginning of an assignment was a difficult period for the children, in which the presence of their parents was equally crucial.

Additionally, many WODs also experienced high levels of guilt when making decision in regards to their children's education.

> The most difficult thing for me was that in [West African country] they did not have high schools for my first son, so I had to leave him in a boarding school, (*looking down*) so that was really hard for me. (Marta, p. 10-11, l. 113-115)

Here, Marta described her two-way guilt by referring to one of the hardest decisions she had to make when she embarked on this journey. Having to leave her son behind, Marta looked down and avoided eye contact with me, suggesting that her feelings of guilt were perhaps combined with a sense of betrayal towards her son. She seems to have experienced this dilemma, as the choice to stay with her son or accompany her husband was both irreconcilable demands.

Lina, who decided to take the children with her, also experienced great remorse when reflecting on the decisions she took on behalf of her children.

> Ow! Up to know it affects me, (slower pace) up to know it affects me. When I think about when we arrived here and there with three children, knowing no one, and their first day of school, this was the hardest part. It affected me and it's affecting me until now... (Lina, p. 23, l. 331-333)

Lina highlighted the effect of imposing her lifestyle on her children. She became emotional when remembering the first moments her children experienced in diplomatic assignments, suggesting that change of school and lack of friends were "the hardest part:"

> (*Tears in her eyes*) when I think about it, until now I get affected by it. Until now my son is 27, my daughter 26, and the small one 22, they are grown up kids and successful. But up to know, when I see them, I see this in their eyes. The children of a diplomat are the one who make the diplomatic life difficult, in that sense. Yeah, this was the most breaking thing for me. Diplomatic life is okay until you think about this. (Lina, p. 23, l. 334-339)

Although Lina's husband was retired at the time of the interview and her children permanently based in different countries, her reflection of the past brought tears to her eyes as she empathized with her children's experience. Lina's pain felt so present and so great that I found myself putting my hands on my heart as she referred to the pain of her children still being visible through their eyes. Her concluding statement suggested an awareness of the main difficulty of diplomatic assignments. Even though she faced many challenges throughout her journey, the only challenge that "broke" her was being a mother on diplomatic assignments. She explained this further:

> Guilt again, and re-questioning things. [...] You know, like, children can have problems even if they stay in the same school

and they don't change countries. But when you take them and they start having problems, you feel guilty. Like if I had stayed in [home country] maybe he wouldn't face all these problems. So children are the biggest stress. (Lina, p. 34-35, l. 495-504)

Lina seemed to take a big part of the responsibility as she acknowledged that her lifestyle had been imposed on her children. Although she projected an awareness that any type of child can experience problems at school, she seemed to infer that she will never know if her children's problems were related to their moves or not. Hence, her guilt was a result of self-questioning that emerged from the doubts she had in regards to her choices:

Children are sensitive and sensible and, uh, you know you impose this life on them so you feel guilty and this breaks you. If you have some breaking moment, this is a breaking moment. When your daughter comes from school and has issues in her social life, this is the real issue with what we do. Even if you are with Obama during the day and the afternoon you come and you child has an issue like that, you forget absolutely everything. You are breaking, you break. This is the issue, the children. (Lina, p. 22, l. 323-329)

Here, Lina used the word "break" to reflect how it felt for her to impose these difficulties on her children. Her example suggested that regardless of one's success as a diplomat or a WOD, the most important aspect will always be one's children. Her word suggested that every positive accomplishment had the power to become banal when the essential happiness of her children was not met.

Another worry was most specifically about the kids. Were they okay? Were they happy? What was best for them? And these questions haunted me. (Louise, p. 46, l. 674-676)

Louise's list of questions showed the intensity of her worries with regard to her children. Her use of the word "haunted" suggested that she was tormented by these questions and that her children occupied a central part in her quality of life considerations.

Elan, on the other hand, described a different kind of guilt when acknowledging that she was educating her children differently from how she had been brought up:

> It was a tough decision, because you know everything was permanent for me, so how am I going to raise my children in this transient life? I felt so bad for not giving them the same stability that I had. (Elan, p. 13, l. 190-192)

Elan expressed a sense of guilt when thinking about her own life prior to having a family. She referred to decisions as being "tough" as she tried to find the right way to bring up her children in "transient" environments. In fact, it seemed as though she was experiencing an internal struggle between how she was raised, in an environment that was permanent, and how she was going to raise her children, in a life rooted in constant change. The unpredictability and uncertainty of the "transient life" appeared to worry Elan, as she expressed fears of not being able to provide them with what they needed:

> I realized after moving from [home country] that everything felt temporary for them, against to how I was brought up. And it's bad because relationships are short, and I was afraid that they would grow up to become adults that can't commit to long-term things, like degrees, relationships. (Elan, p. 32, l. 474-477)

Elan appeared to be aware of some of the consequences of experiencing a lack of stability. She expressed fears of not giving her children a healthy environment in which they could potentially develop into healthy adults, as they seemed to lack the notion of long-term commitments. This sense of impermanence seemed to preoccupy Elan's mind, as she realized how permanence and stability were important factors that had helped her develop into the woman she was.

> You know, we decided to put them in this situation, so the least we could do is to make sure they are taken care of well and that their needs are met at all time. (Elan, p. 46, l. 682-683)

As a mother, Elan took responsibility for the situation in which she had put her children. She appeared to work very hard in making amends to them, as her sense of responsibility seemed to carry an element of culpability.

As expressed by most participants, this sub-theme showed how being a mother during diplomatic assignments was the main challenge WODs face. Their sense of guilt and constant self-doubt were at the root of how they felt about themselves and their experiences. The next sub-theme describes how participants felt as they experienced the pressures of creating new homes.

3.3.3   Pressure to Create a New Home

Throughout their interviews, many WODs talked at length about their duties towards their families. It often seemed that many administrative roles would fall on them, as well as their responsibilities to create a new home in every country, for themselves and their children.

Lina talked about the different responsibilities she had in her first diplomatic assignment:

> It was difficult to manage all of this. Like learning about [important North American city], manage the children, do activities, make sure to find the right doctors. So, like, the administrative part was very demanding. And it's like that (slower pace) **every time we move**. (Lina, p. 27, l. 391-393)

Here, Lina seemed to experience difficulties in managing the different duties she had. She understood that her role was of high importance because her children depended on her. Lina appeared to highlight two important elements that differentiated her from other mothers, however: the importance of learning about the new host country, and that she had to repeat all these duties every time they were assigned to a new host country. She ended her statement in a very slow monotone, suggesting memories of fatigue and boredom in repeating these tasks.

In the same way, Amy described her administrative duties when she and her family would start a new assignment:

> The husband goes straight to work, and for him it was very clear you have something on your table to eat, and he has a job schedule, whereas for me I need to know where to shop, which school to put them, learn the language and the traditions of the country, know who to contact to organize the events, train the staff, take care of my children **AND** be there with my husband. (Amy, p. 22, l. 321-326)

Amy emphasized on the difference between her husband's role and her own when moving to a new country. She described her husband's perception of his duties as going to work and making money. When comparing his duties to hers, she enumerated a series of responsibilities to which she needed to attend when starting a new assignment. Each duty also seemed to be about taking care of her children, her husband, and the job, suggesting that little space was left for self-care.

Elan also talked about how it felt to be a part of these postings. She explained that diplomatic assignments were extremely demanding as a WOD, as everybody needed a part of her:

> And it's like, ouf, how much can I teach my children our culture, and how much can I be there for my husband, and do my work, and host. Haha it seems like a lot to do! (Elan, p. 37, l. 550-553)

Elan's pressure to achieve different things was felt through the use of enumeration and repeating "and" four times. She started her list with an onomatopoeic reaction "ouf," illustrating her overwhelming responsibilities. She followed this onomatopoeia with a rhetorical question: "How much can I..." in order to illuminate the difficulties in conducting every task in a perfect way. Elan's nervous laugh "Haha" and comment "it seems like a lot to do!" illustrated how unreasonable the demands were for her to be able to perfect them all.

> The diplomatic life is already unstructured, and our government is unstructured, and in all of this, they ask of us that we be structured and stable. They ask for the impossible, but we have to manage anyway. (Caline, p. 30, l. 439-442)

Caline's statement went to the heart of her experience of being a WOD, as she is greatly affected by the fact that represented a country that was political, economically, and socially unstable. She referred to the diplomatic world and to her government as unstable and chaotic, suggesting that as a WOD she was only bound to feel unstable and chaotic herself. However, she highlighted the irony of her role by showing how other's expected from her to always remain "structured and stable," while not allowing her to fall down:

> You have to keep a structure somewhere but at the same time you are completely torn apart. (Caline, p. 31, l. 448-449)

Caline emphasized the "structure" she had to keep in order to let others believe that everything was under control, while in reality she was "completely torn apart." This fake façade seemed to be affecting her quality of life, suggesting that she was suffering in silence.

Some WODs described how their role was essential by explaining the importance of their ability to make decisions that helped the family feel comfortable and safe in these new environments.

But you know the children and my husband left for me to choose, again. 'You choose, you decide which school we should go to.' So again the burden fell on me. (Elan, p. 32, l. 472-474)

The burden falls again on me every time. (Elan, p. 33, l. 480-481)

Elan described how her husband and children relied on her to make one of the most important and difficult decisions when being on diplomatic assignments, namely choosing the right school. This decision seemed to hold a lot of stress as many factors came into play. Elan referred to this decision as a "burden," suggesting that it had a mental heaviness to it.

In other instances, Elan felt the need to create a family environment for her children. She explained her decision in this way:

In every assignment, I always made the decision that we surround ourselves with people from our country. I told my husband that I want our children and ourselves to feel like a part of our country is here with us. So we would invite our friends all the time, like even now, after the interview my husband is bringing an officer to have lunch here. I like that. I created that thing so they always felt also that there are always people in our home. So I created that family environment everywhere we went. (Elan, p. 41, l. 610-616)

Elan's attempt to create a family environment suggested her profound need to compensate for the lack of familiarity and permanence she had discussed earlier. Her decision to create a family abroad and have people from their home country in their house showed Elan's willingness to create a sense of home everywhere they went. She appeared to have created and instilled traditions that she practiced in every assignment, leaving her family to experience a sense of sameness.

I decided that we needed to meet people from [home country] who had children the same age as mine. So we became closer with a few couples because of the children and we had like our little family in [Important North American City]. (Amy, p. 26, l. 380-383)

Similarly, Amy felt a need to meet other families of similar background. Her active decision to help her children and husband develop profound relationships with others seemed to stem from her need to provide them with an extended family, one they would usually have in their home country. Amy also experienced this need given the emphasis that her culture puts on family and community ties.

Other participants, such as Marta, discussed practical ways they instilled this sense of sameness for themselves and their families.

> For each assignment, I decided to bring some furniture with me, so I have, uh, to feel at home, I have some tips like my bed with this picture, in my house, behind these sofas, I put exactly these two paintings, doesn't matter where I am in the world, it is the same. So that whenever we come home and open the door, we see these and say "Ah ok I am home!" and not feel like we are in a hotel (Marta, p. 29, l. 327-331)

Marta's decision to follow a specific routine when moving houses seemed to have left her and her family with a sense of relief. Her statement suggested that she easily felt homesick on postings as her home was not her home. However, her practical "tips" appeared to have brought her and her family comfort, safety, and stability.

This master theme dealt with the way WODs perceived their family roles during diplomatic assignments. Their ability to have positive attitudes has been at the center of their journey and has allowed them to cope with the expectations of others. This section also highlighted various challenges and demands put upon them and how they affected their quality of life.

The next and final master theme will deal with WODs confusing their identities and their ability to make sense of their presence in these postings.

3.4   Master Theme 4 – Making Sense of Who I Am and Who I Want to Be

This last master theme focused on the evolution of WODs throughout their diplomatic journeys. It seemed to reflect on the loss of the person they were but also highlighted the person they had strived to become. In the first sub-theme, "Who Am I in this New World?," WODs appeared to reflect on their new identities and what it initially meant for them. The second sub-theme, "Making Sense of my Presence," focused on the different ways WODs made sense of their new identities and how they came across. In the final sub-theme, "the Need for Personal Success," WODs seemed to have come to the conclusion that their role in these assignments was important and recognition was crucial.

3.4.1   Who Am I in this New World?

Some participants experienced identity threats in which they were unable to understand who they were in their husbands' diplomatic assignments. This confusing transition left them with many doubts and questions, as expressed by Elan:

> It was so difficult for me to understand this. I asked myself why are you here? In what capacity are you here? The reason? You are not here in holidays, you are not a tourist, you are here on a diplomatic passport, representing your country. (Elan, p. 26, l. 381-384)

Elan's intense self-questioning showed her active process of reflection. Indeed, she tried to understand in what capacity was she in this new country. As she attempted to make sense of her presence, she seemed to have reflected on her residential status, suggesting that it helped her deal better with her confusion. As she identified her diplomatic passport as the main reason for her presence, she understood that her role in this new country was purely one of representation.

Becoming a WOD was a new identity that came with feelings of doubt about who Elan really was. She commented that before becoming a WOD, she had a clearer and more solid sense of herself. This changed drastically, leading to a deep sense of identity loss:

> When we went in [South Asian country], I thought I was going to study and it didn't work out, so I was thinking what am I going to do, what is my role, my future? He had his life set but it was mine that was unknown. (Elan, p. 36, l. 530-532)

Elan explained having embarked on this journey with a plan, and perhaps the possibility of coming to this first assignment with the same sense of self that she had back home. Her experience of losing her identity brought many questions about who she was. As her husband experienced his self-identity in a more stable way, Elan tried to make sense of the doubts she was having:

> I decided to join him but it never occurred to me if I could do this so I went through a difficult period, I'm just a wife, can I do this all my life? What's going to happen to me? (Elan, p. 36, l. 532-534)

This account demonstrated Elan's ability to make sense of her presence in these missions. The use of the phrase "I decided to join him, but" showed her ability to recognize that although she decided to join her husband in his missions, her choice was not fully informed. Moreover, Elan experienced some identity threat as she did not know if she would ever be able to "just be a wife." Her use of the word "just" illustrated her own perception of what it was for her to be a WOD. She seeming to devalue the role of being a wife, as many facets of her new identity were still unknown to her. The fear of this new identity threat was also revealed by her question of "what's going to happen to me," illustrating her insecurity in regards to self-concept.

Elan later tried to make sense of her identity, which resulted in an attempt at understanding who she was:

> With us like we are not tourists, we have residents, not for too long, but still we live there. And when you are an expat or diplomat, you know it's for a little while, you learn that the bad things will be over when you leave, and the good things you try and make the most out of it ... So it's a good thing, because you take what's good and leave what's bad. (Elan, p. 34, l. 496-500)

Elan still expressed puzzlement about her identity, as she lived in a foreign country under specific residency terms. She was not a tourist, nor was she a long-term resident, which seemed to make her comfortable with the fact that she was there "for a little while." In thinking "you take what's good and leave what's bad," she appeared to be able to make sense of the good and difficult aspects of her short-term stays. Her use of the pronouns "us" and "we" in her first sentence suggested a sense of belonging.

Participants who married men of different nationalities expressed the need to let go of a part of their own identities, in order to let another one in.

> I am [South American nationality]. I had to learn this new culture and act like [her husband's nationality] myself, because I was in [Central West Africa] representing [her husband's country], not [her own country]. So I had to learn about the culture, the language, the people, and do like [her husband's countrymen] do. I feel like my [own] nationality had to disappear a little so I can make place for this new me. (Marta, p. 10, l. 109-113)

Marta explained how being a foreign spouse meant that she had "to let go" of her own national identity in order to assume a new one.

Marta's replacement in national identities seemed to be a challenging one as she was asked to represent a country that was not her own. She referred to her new national identity as part of a "new [her]," suggesting that a part of her had to change as she became a WOD.

> I have no more the [Middle Eastern] passport because when I married my husband, he has the [European nationality] and in his country you cannot have two different nationalities, so I had to give up mine in order to take his because I am representing his country now, not mine. (Ava, p. 3, l. 34-36)

Similarly, Ava described having to give up her passport and her nationality in order to take on her husband's. Her use of the pronouns "his" and "mine" show how different both Ava and her husband are, and yet, how similar they need to be when representing [European country] abroad.

Other WODs spoke about the difficulty in understanding their identities once their husbands retired and their status as WODs disappeared.

> A very difficult thing is when you move back to your home country [...] It's as if for years you have taken on a role and then poof! When your husband retires, it's as if you become nobody when you go back to your home country. It's difficult. (Louise, p. 46, l. 685-690)

Here, Louise referred to the difficulty of transitioning from WOD to the wife of an ex-diplomat. It seemed as though her whole identity depended on her husband's profession, and once his profession ceased to exist, her identity was threatened. Her onomatopoeic reaction, "poof," illustrated the disappearance of a pioneering element to her identity.

Likewise, Amy described coming to her home country as one of the most difficult challenges she had to experience:

> Coming back to [home country] was so depressing for me. For all these years I had a role and I was doing something. I then came

back when my husband retired and found myself not working, not doing anything…(pause)…I never tell anyone this but I was not doing well at all at the time because I couldn't cope. (Amy, p. 43, l. 601-604)

Amy's confession seemed to be one that was difficult to admit. By referring to her husband's retirement, her paralinguistics revealed that something bad had happened to her when she lost her identity of WOD. It seemed as if her identity had been threatened again, suggesting that she needed to find herself again. Her long pause showed the difficulty of admitting the extent of this challenge, as she "couldn't cope" with these feelings of emptiness.

While this sub-theme dealt with the different identity threats WODs experienced, the next sub-theme will focus on the different ways in which participants made sense of their presence and coped with their roles as WOD.

3.4.2   Making Sense of My Presence

This sub-theme dealt with the various strategies WODs used to accept their presence and roles in diplomatic assignments. For some, making sense of their presence grew through their sense of usefulness in diplomatic duties.

Lina, for example, raised awareness of the way she mattered in her husband's diplomatic work:

I was friends with very important people, wives of important people. And you know, this is how you help your husband. You help by befriending others and building important and strong relationships. Because when you do that, you then invite the wife and husband, and then help your husband in networking and meeting important people. And I mean, this is how the diplomatic world works. It works by having contacts and doing change. And how can you do change when you don't know anybody. So by being friends with the wives, you help both husbands build a relationship. And this is what I did. (Lina, p. 10, l. 148-155)

Lina seemed to have experienced her presence with her husband as an essential element in his diplomatic career. She conveyed an understanding of what diplomatic assignments are for her, namely networking and "doing change," and explained that these activities can only be done when knowing others. Lina described her sense of triumph by recognizing the importance of her role in helping her husband meet important people and creating the network he needed to conduct his work. From her language and non-verbal communication, Lina seemed proud of her accomplishments, as she understood her purpose in these assignments. She praised herself for knowing "important people" and being able to provide an added element to her husband's work by networking in a way that he wouldn't be able to do on his own.

I gave my 100%, and at the time I also felt that by doing this I would help my husband climb the ladder, because the wife plays an important role by pleasing the people and showing that you are a good host and that I could take care of others in that sense (Ava, p. 19, l. 269-272)

Similarly, Ava experienced her role as needing to "please" others in order to diplomatically help her husband. She seemed to link her contribution and involvement in diplomatic assignments as a direct element to help her "husband climb the ladder." Ava's willingness to please others and proving them that she was good appeared to directly affect her sense of purpose and experience of her role. By acknowledging that "the wife plays an important role," she emphasized on the concept of usefulness and experienced her role as complementary to her husband's, suggesting that her absence would have affected the assignment.

Sarah also explained how her role became diplomatically important:

> We hosted big cocktails but it is your responsibility to make sure that everybody's happy, and drinking and make conversation with everyone. So while others are having fun, I am on duty. (Sarah, p. 21, l. 296-298)

Here, Sarah acknowledged that hosting cocktails was a team effort. However, she seemed to specify that it was mainly her responsibility to assure other's happiness and enjoyment of the party, suggesting that it was only then that she felt that she became diplomatically useful. The end of her quote suggested that although others were there for leisure, for her, it was part of her diplomatic duties.

In other instances, some WODs experienced their diplomatic duties by meeting others' expectations of their role:

> The wife of the ambassador expected so much from me because it was such a busy city for us. Every month we would receive ministerial delegations and like we had to host all the time the wives of the prime minister and other ministers. [ ] I had to make sure that breakfast went accordingly, wait for them at eight in the morning for them to come down, take them shopping to the best places, make sure they were happy, and you know, even if I had my own life going on, and my children, everything needed to be put on hold because it was my duty to attend to their needs. (Elan, p. 23, l. 338-347)

Elan's experience of having to meet others' expectations was one that came with great diplomatic pressure. She expressed this pressure by enumerating the different tasks she was given when she was on duty. Although Elan's experience seemed to emphasize the different roles she had to play to make others happy, the real emphasis was on the obligation she experienced having to put her own life on hold for diplomatic reasons.

Her comment suggested that no real importance was given to her or her needs when diplomatic expectations were put upon her

> In [North American Country] the wife of diplomat is supposed to play a role. People expect that from her. So like in her husband career and his life. So for me that role was social, cultural mainly. (Lina, p. 3, l. 34-36)

Here, Lina also described the expectations that locals had of her. Her tone at the time suggested that she felt like she did not have a choice and that being involved in her husband's work was the only way her identity could be validated by others.

In contrast, other WODs described the need to go the extra mile in order to make sense of their presence. Some experienced personal aspirations in regard to their own personal lives and decided to either merge them or split them from their husband's postings. Caline, for instance, decided to merge her passion for teaching with her diplomatic duties:

> I really tried to mix my passion for teaching in our assignments, like when we were in [North America] I decided to put in a program where we would teach children the language, the culture, our national anthem, and you know, this helped me feel like I had a purpose. I am of use and that was important for me. (Caline, p. 28, l. 408-412)

Caline described feeling useful as she brought an element to the diplomatic assignments that resonated with the person she was before diplomatic postings. In fact, Caline taught languages in a prestigious university and expressed throughout the interview her love and success in teaching languages. She talked at length about the worries of her community, as they were complaining about their children's unfamiliarity with the home country's official language. It seemed that Caline felt it was her duty to help local children reconnect with their native country while serving her community.

Similarly, Louise found herself merging her love for writing with diplomatic assignments:

> This wife had a really bad time during their posting and she told me that I should use my passion and write about our experiences as trailing spouses. So that's what I did and I wrote two books about my experiences as a trailing spouse and they became bestsellers! And you know…I couldn't have done that without my husband's postings. (Louise, p. 21, l. 302-305)

Louise seemed grateful to have taken part in diplomatic assignments. She confessed that her success wouldn't have been possible and that diplomatic postings gave her an opportunity to become a successful writer. In her experience, she described having met women who confided in her and gave her the responsibility to give WODs a voice. Given Louise's background in journalism, she seemed to have been able to find her vocation and merge her love for writing with her role in the diplomatic world.

Sarah, likewise, experienced instances where she was able to find her place in diplomatic assignments:

> With this blog and these articles that I had been writing from an anthropological perspective…also from the [Middle East], I think my motivation is to spread knowledge about the Middle East to [home country], because so little is written and it's always about the same issues, the negative things, so I kind of want to give, uh, perspective and feelings from the ground. (Sarah, p. 20-21, l. 272-276)

Sarah appeared to have been able to merge her anthropological interests with diplomatic postings. She used her exposure to raise awareness and "spread knowledge," suggesting that she perceived her presence in diplomatic assignments as an opportunity to educate others. Having a goal and an interest seemed important for Sarah, as it helped her make sense of her presence.

On the other hand, both Sarah and Marta also described how they aspired to become the people they wanted to be by separating themselves from diplomatic assignments. In fact, although Sarah found herself at times merging both, she also felt the need to have her own separate identity through activities she would do on her own:

> I wrote about our life, where we went, like this, more like cultural things, posting nice photos, but never about my husband's work because I made the decision that this is not about the embassy or diplomatic or the guests of the ministers who are visiting from [Northern European country] but this is about my life (Sarah, p. 20, l. 261-265)

Sarah appeared to make a separation between the person she was in diplomatic postings and her own person. Her creation of a personal blog in which no diplomatic material was posted showed a need to separate herself from her husband's posting. This blog may also have been a way to show others that her identity did not reside solely as being the wife of a diplomat, but that she defined herself as a wife, a traveler, and a writer.

Marta also expressed during our interview how she made a lot of efforts to separate her diplomatic duties from the person she aimed to be:

> At the beginning, it was a sacrifice, but since I discovered the bridge and I had to study it with a partner, it was no longer a sacrifice. It became a challenge and that's what I wanted [...] I remember taking the bridge as a challenge and I made a lot of friends through this from inside and outside embassies (Marta, p. 21, l. 236-243)

Repeatedly, Marta expressed how taking on bridge first felt like a sacrifice, but then shifted to being her personal challenge. Her decision to dedicate herself to bridge suggested a great need to have her own personal challenge during these diplomatic assignments. Also, not only did bridge become a personal challenge, but it also became the vessel that helped her create a social circle, suggesting that through bridge, she felt like she belonged:

> I look at this as a job, not as my life. My life is bridge, the GRS, my children and my marriage. (Marta, p. 39, l. 450-451)

Marta further explained how she perceived her diplomatic role as a separate entity from her identity. She saw diplomatic postings as part of her life, rather than her life. She went on to list the most important things that form her life and her identity, suggesting a sense of thriving through each posting.

Ava also talked about the importance to have a separate identity that was complementary to being a WOD:

> This is very important. This is very important...to have, especially now. Before it was easier for a woman to be only with her husband, but now no. Now her identity needs to be different. She needs to work and have her own identity. (Ava, p. 13, l. 180-183)

Ava's repetition of "this is very important" highlighted the significance of having a separate identity. She compared women from different generations to show the shift in the importance for an independent self-concept, suggesting a recognition that self-actualization is more important for today's generation.

On the other hand, some WODs made sense of their presence in each assignment by striving at their role, rather than thriving. Elan, for instance, talked at length about how she felt that she had no possibility of disappointing others, leading her to make sense of her presence and to perfect her role:

> So when I realized that they were disappointed and felt like it was a waste, I decided that if this is what I'm going to do, then I will perfect at it and give it my best. (Elan, p. 17, l. 243-244)

Elan referred to her parent's disappointment in her for "just being a wife." As a result, she decided to take on this role and strive at it as it was the only way she could prove to others and herself that her identity as a WOD was valid. She continued by providing another detailed account of a situation where her performance needed to be faultless:

> When it's the president's wife or the minister's wife, you can't say you don't know, never say that because then it seems like you are not doing your part. You have to know. (Elan, p. 17, l. 251-253)

The way Elan talked about the absolute necessity to "know" indicated what appeared to be an element of fear of not knowing and a need to strive. She commented saying "never say that," which suggested the possibility of severe consequences such as being labeled as "not doing your part," suggesting a threat to her WOD identity. Moreover, Elan stood somewhat in a position in which her marriage also depended on the way she made sense of her presence:

> I will perfect at it and give it my best. I'll make the best out of it and only then I realized that if I want to keep my marriage from breaking, I have to be like this and embrace the diplomatic life. (Elan, p. 18, l. 266-268)

Elan suggested that the only way to have a healthy and stable marriage was to embrace her duties as a WOD and base her identity upon that role. Here, she seemed to understand that accepting the need to strive was the only way to cope with the lifestyle and keep her marriage from "breaking."

Amy explained how striving came naturally for her given that she admired her husband's job:

> I liked his job. I wouldn't choose it for myself, but I liked what he was doing, and how he was doing it, so I admired what he did. So maybe that was my motivation to get more engaged with him and be really, really good. So this is why it felt natural for me. (Amy, p. 31, l. 443-445)

Amy explained how her motivation at striving as a WOD came from her admiration of her husband and her liking for the diplomatic field. It seemed like her choice to engage was one she made intentionally, suggesting a congruency in her identity. Amy expanded on the power of choice and explained how it impacted her views on her presence:

> Because at the beginning it was I am doing this for you, but then it was not fair, because it was my choice to join him, he never forced me to join, I decided to. And I realized that if I keep on thinking that I am doing this for him and his career, our marriage will not last long because it is very detrimental. (Amy, p. 35, l. 509-512)

Amy's understanding of her active decision-making seemed to have helped her make sense of her presence. By highlighting the power of choice, she appeared to have shifted her views on why and for whom she was doing all these efforts, and understood that these negative feelings could have potentially impacted her marriage.

> This is also making the choice that if you have chosen this then concentrate on the positive things and of course be aware of the negative things. (Sarah, 48, l. 702-704)

Sarah explained how having a choice helped her maintain an optimistic attitude towards her role in this journey. Her statements also suggested how she was coming to terms with her presence and coped by focusing on the positive things.

Louise explained this further by explaining how she managed the difficulties.

> I just kept in my mind the funny things, or the things I most liked (laughing), but that's it. So I always managed to…I think so. (Louise, 58, l. 675-676)

Louise identified humor as a good way to manage the difficulties. Throughout her interview, she laughed about stories or difficult moments she experienced in the past, suggesting that she was able to see the good in these experiences and learn from the bad.

> I also saw it as an opportunity and like I knew that it was just for a few years, so I really tried to enjoy it as much as I can and have fun in every posting. (Amy, p. 52, l. 702-704)

Amy explained how she tried to make sense of her postings and how her perception of them as opportunities helped her manage the difficult times. Her awareness that this lifestyle was only temporary helped her enjoy it further, as the concept of their finiteness seemed to be vividly in her mind.

Other WODs talked about shifting their perceptions on diplomatic postings. Both Ava and Caline mention this change:

> I think that's how I managed mostly, by knowing that I was doing things for the both of us, because his success equaled my success. (Ava, p. 54, l. 784-785)

> At the beginning it was 'I'm doing this for you and only for you;' it felt like I was sacrificing myself for him. But with time the 'doing it for YOU became doing it for US.' (Caline, p. 40, l. 580-584)

Both WODs expressed how their sense of togetherness helped them come to terms with their presence in diplomatic assignments. Their notion of success seemed to be anchored in the "we" concept, and actions that were once perceived as solely done for "him" were now conducted for "their" joint success.

Elan and Sarah, on the other hand, explained how being congruent within themselves helped them manage the diplomatic life.

> You need to be your own best friend. As you move, you will have a lot of friends, but you will not have this one best friend. [...] So you need to be your own best friend. At night you face your own conscious so you need to be friends with yourself, love yourself. So find ways to enjoy yourself and to take care of yourself. (Elan, p. 44, l. 642-646)

Elan described how being in harmony within herself was crucial in order to make sense of her presence and get through this journey. She referred to being her own best friend, suggesting that she was at peace with her self-image, and that self-care was highly important.

Sarah explained how her need to prove herself was not a priority anymore:

> I'm old enough, I made already a long career, I had many demanding jobs in [home country], I think I didn't need to prove anymore that I can make it so I could afford to jump to being just a wife (Sarah, p. 11, l. 138-141)

She also expressed how congruent she was with herself, as she had let go of the need to prove herself. Her statement suggested that her self-esteem was quite high, as she was not affected by others perception of her as "just a wife." In a way, her life long career seemed to have helped her form the base for a solid identity that appeared to not be easily affected by others.

In drawing the various strands of this sub-theme together, participants' experiences of making sense of their presence were interpreted in ways that have profound implications for how they experienced their role and identity throughout diplomatic postings. As all WODs found themselves diplomatically involved, some embraced their duties and roles and used them to construct their identities, while others viewed it as only a part of who they are. In the final sub-theme, WODs explored their thoughts and feelings as they realized the importance of personal successes.

3.4.3   The Need for Personal Success

In this sub-theme, WODs appeared to reflect on the importance of having some form of personal success in diplomatic assignments. Some expressed national pride in representing their countries abroad and experienced their role as a dedication to their countries. Recognition of their efforts helped WODs understand who they aspired to be in diplomatic posting and facilitated the process in which their identities changed.

Sarah, who referred to herself as a civil servant during the interview, explained how she viewed her role in regards to her country:

> I also value the work of diplomats, [...] so it's my personal expression of course that I'm willing to give my years, not my life, but my years to serving my country and I really think that I am serving my country as well, even though I'm not paid for this. (Sarah, p. 55, l. 740-744)

Here, Sarah showed her dedication to her country. It seemed as if she perceived her duty towards her country as independent of her husband's profession and showed willingness to offer some "years" of service to her country. The end of her statement showed how Sarah drew on a similarity with her husband by the use of "as well." Her interjection of "even though" showed a sense of inequality, as Sarah did not get paid for representing and giving her years to her country, compared to her husband.

> You know, I work so hard for my country. I don't care who is in my country governing, but I did it for my country. (Lina, p. 10, l. 134-135)

Lina expressed pride in representing her country and working for it. During the interview, her paralinguistics suggested a real sense of accomplishment. Similar to Sarah, Lina also appeared to experience this duty towards her country independently from her husband's profession, as her national involvement was also highlighted by her disinterest in who governed her country.

Other WODs talked at length about the importance of being recognized by others. Their need for recognition seemed to be anchored in their desire for validity and acknowledgment that their presence did make a change:

> At the end of the day, you want recognition because you were part of the success. (Louise p. 52, l. 721)

Louise reflected on how her role in these postings led to success. She affirmed wanting to be appreciated for her efforts, suggesting that it was only then that her role was validated.

Lina explained this further:

> I think as a woman, if you don't make them feel your presence, you have to make sure to remind them that you are here and that you exist and that you are doing many things. I mean as a woman, uh, they always have to take you into account. Your husband, your children and other people always have to make sure that you are here. You always have to remind them not to take you for granted in what you are doing. Reminding them that you know I did this, I did that, because sometimes they like to take the credit and you are in a men's world don't forget, so you always have to remind them where the credit belongs. (Lina, p. 29, l. 413-420)

Lina took a stand while explaining her need for recognition. She referred to the importance of doing so as a woman, given her experience of women being unrecognized and having to fight for acknowledgment of their accomplishments. She referred to being present in a "man's world," suggesting that she was aware that all forms of power and dominance belonged to them not only in the diplomatic world, but also in her family system and culture. Lina expressed a need to fight this patriarchal system, suggesting that a part of her felt the narrative needed to change and her place in workforce needed to be clear:

> At the end of the day, you want to be recognized because you were part of the success. (Lina, p. 29, l. 428)

Lina reaffirmed her position by explaining why her need for recognition was important. Her logic seemed to convey the clarity and simplicity of a cause-effect situation in which being "part of the success" should only result in appreciation for the efforts put in place.

Amy, on the other hand, expressed a sense of achievement through the way diplomatic assignments made her feel about herself:

> I mean, I became a lot more confident. I mean, this is where I realized how much I can do. I felt like I am capable of doing many things. Like before assignments I was working but it was very narrow so it didn't give me the confidence that I needed. But in these assignments, I discovered more my skills and realized that I can do many things that I am good at. (Amy, p. 16, l. 238-241)

Here, Amy described how diplomatic postings increased her self-esteem in terms of discovering abilities. She experienced a different version of herself, suggesting that the diplomatic context helped her grow and develop her personal potential. Her realization of "how much [she] can do" seemed to be a crucial element of how Amy experienced her sense of self. This is also how she made sense of who she became through these postings and what she took from these experiences in regard to her self-esteem.

Finally, Elan expressed how she experienced her sense of achievement:

> I want to feel that I have achieved something in 20 years. I feel good about myself now because I know I have achieved. And I did not have to do any of it I did it for my own initiative. (Elan, p. 31, l. 453-455)

As Elan reflected on her sense of self, she expressed having reached a state where she felt "good about [her]self," suggesting that pride and contempt were at the center of her experience. Looking back, Elan stated that she "now" felt good about herself as she came to the realization that all of her achievements were self-driven by the potential she had, suggesting that perhaps she felt like she had reached a state of self-actualization.

This final master theme has explored WODs senses of self by questioning their own personal identities and then coming to terms with the woman they each hoped to become. Although there was a rich contrast and divergence in the accounts within these sub-themes, all WODs expressed a need to strive, thrive, achieve, and/or matter, suggesting a desire to become congruent with their ideal-selves.

3.5   Brief Summary of Findings

WODs seemed to experience a continuous process of making sense of their presence and their identities while accompanying their husbands on diplomatic assignments. It felt that their togetherness and partnership with their husbands became solid ground that allowed them to manage their loss of self. Indeed, within their stable and supportive marriages, they experienced a great identity threat of which they spent much time trying to make sense so that they could come to the conclusion of who they truly are as WODs. However, this process felt quite circular at times as many obstacles, such as raising their children in a transient environment, were experienced throughout their journey, leaving WODs to experience constant a threat to and reconstruction of who they are and what their purpose is.

Chapter 4 - Discussion

In this section, I will provide a tentative model of the inter-relationship between themes and present an overview of the analysis, creating a "bird's eye view" of WODs' experiences. Then, I will consider the main findings in terms of their relations to the existing literature and theory. The following section will critically appraise the research in terms of quality markers for qualitative research and transferability, which the reader should bear in mind when evaluating the significance of this project. I will also consider the contributions the findings make to the field of counseling psychology in terms of research and practice. Lastly, I will highlight some future areas for research and present some concluding notes and reflections.

4.1 Overview of the Analysis

In an attempt to understand what is the experience of being a WOD, the participants engaged in a process of self-exploration and reflection touching upon this phenomenon. The analysis strived to capture and bring to light this detailed exploration. Figure 2 represents a diagrammatic depiction of this thematic model.

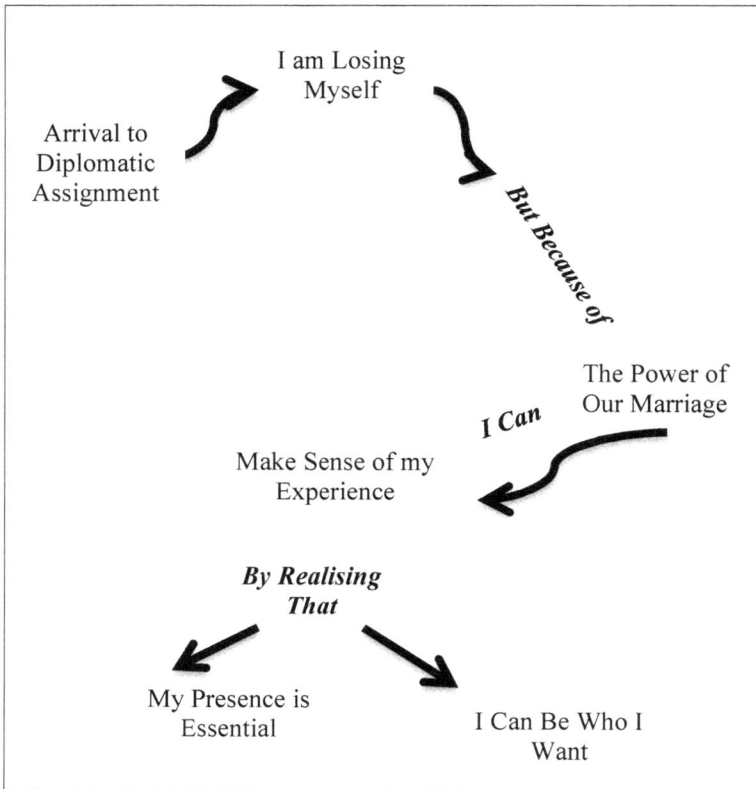

Figure 2: Diagrammatic Representation of the Findings

The diverse sociocultural backgrounds of the participants (Middle Eastern, European, South Asian, and South American), and their husbands' countries of origin and employment status, all contributed to the different experiences of the WODs under study. Nevertheless, as shown by the master themes, all eight participants shared many commonalities in their experiences. I will provide an overview of these similarities and contrasts, and attempt to show how they intersect.

For all participants, it seemed that having a good and stable marriage was absolutely crucial in their experience. They identified love for their husbands as the main reason for embarking on their journeys. Many claimed that love was not only a trigger but also the main reason to stay in diplomatic assignments and to attend to some responsibilities as a couple. Some WODs talked at length about their experiences of being part of a team with their husbands. This sense of togetherness proved quite important, as it helped them feel that they were side-by-side with their husbands, rather than standing behind. This sense of belonging to the job was also experienced by some WODs who described their husbands' emotional support as crucial to their well-being, as it provided them a sense of being understood and accounted for.

Most WODs described life during diplomatic assignments as challenging, especially during the first postings, with some even referring to a loss of self. Some experienced a sense of alienation as they realized that their lives would be centered around their husbands' careers, leading them to doubt their identities and senses of purpose. Their doubt and confusion with regard to who they are seemed to have created a strong internal threat due to the core nature, salience, and importance of this identity. This might mean that in their search for a new purpose, they were faced with negative and frightening feelings about what their lives were going to be.

In their attempts to make meaning of this experience, some participants displayed many non-verbal cues suggesting frustration with their inability to control major life decisions, such as choosing the next host country. Being a WOD, from this perspective, seemed to imply a fragile, and sometimes even absent sense of presence, with little or no place to be one's full self.

The question of choice and control over the decision to embark on this journey seemed to be a very important factor in the way WODs interpreted and perceived their situations. All of them reported that it had been their own decision to assist their husbands, although many did not know what to expect from their new lives. Their ability to take responsibility for the lives they chose seemed to allow them to accept the challenges they experienced.

This sense of choice and control was, unfortunately, not experienced when seven of the eight WODs discussed their roles as mothers of diplomatic children. Their helplessness was amplified when it dawned on them that they had imposed this lifestyle upon their children. This situation held many implications for their senses of self as they experienced guilt and remorse when thinking about their inability to be there as a mother while wanting to be present with their husbands on a full-time basis.

One marked consequence of holding multiple identity components was a sense of doubt, guilt, confusion, and ambivalence. These feelings of instability were not only expressed explicitly, but were also insinuated through participants' non-verbal communication during the interview, particularly when a difficult experience was being shared and participants were not able to articulate some of their feelings effectively. Some WODs engaged in a back-and-forth process, in which they expressed good feelings and optimistic views, while at other times expressing negative feelings for similar situations. These conflicted feelings might suggest that one key components of being a WOD is this lack of solidity or "solid ground." Interestingly, WODs experience their lifestyles in the same manner they expressed their meaning-making, namely as an unstable, ambivalent, and conflicting experience.

Some WODs mentioned the difficulty of belonging in a society where diplomats and their spouses were perceived to be different. Some stated that diplomats were asked to talk about serious topics and to use their intellectual abilities in conversations, whereas spouses were asked to always engage in superficial topics, which made them feel that they were regressing intellectually. This separation affected many WODs' psyches, leading them to feel that their presence was shallow and even irrelevant at times, as they did not have any space to be themselves.

Participants attempted to manage these experiences in diverse ways. On the intra-psychic level, some WODs seemed to find it useful to redefine the concepts at the core of the identity struggle, namely their roles and purposes in their postings. This possibly implied a major shift in the way they made meaning of major elements of their experiences as WODs, which allowed them to have the possibility of revising their identities. These were mainly experienced as striving or thriving in diplomatic assignments. Some WODs decided to become perfect at their roles, while others accepted that it was their husbands' job, but that their lives were about other activities.

These strategies could be seen as an attempt to create positive distinctiveness and self-esteem by changing the meaning WODs attached to their status and experiences of self. Nonetheless, these attempts were partially successful, with some WODs experiencing doubts, guilt, and uncertainty. Indeed, some of these attempts at managing their identity felt circular, as WODs seemed to experience themselves differently depending on their children's well-being, the proximity of the host country to the home country, their quality of life, and levels of "busyness" in their host countries.

Finally, other attempts at management included avoidance and absence, which some participants described as an oxygenation period in which they would travel to a different city or country in order to breathe and re-energize before returning to the posting. Some WODs also noted taking years off, by not accompanying their husband to a certain posting, so that they could focus on themselves or on their children.

4.2 Significant Findings and Contributions

In this section, the project's findings will be located within the existing literature and theory in relation to the themes discussed in Chapter Three. First, I will discuss how the analysis and findings add to the current literature for WOD. I will then explore how the findings apply to the theories of identity discussed in the first chapter, with a specific focus on Identity Process Theory and Theory of the Self. I will utilize these two theories to provide a useful framework to understand how being a WOD is experienced. In the following sections, I will develop on the different ways in which these theories can contribute to the field of counseling psychology and the potential implications they could have for research and practice.

4.2.1. WODs and the Literature

WODs struggle from frequent relocations in an already inherently and uniquely stressful way of life. They have reported feeling lost, unimportant, and anxious about their futures (Arieli, 2007; Cangià, 2018; Collins & Bertone, 2017). In the context of these experiences, Cangià's (2018) recent study indicated the unpredictability of diplomatic postings as a source of uncertainty, leading women to experience feelings of insecurity and precarity. She explains further that the transition to unemployment, particularly, can destabilize the accompanying spouse's identity, as she needs to reconsider her self-concept in this new environment (Cangià, 2018). Cangià (2018) finally explains how spouses can reconfigure their identities within a marriage in order to make sense of their senses of self and precarious feelings.

This study validates Cangià's (2018) claim that the first channel for identity reconfiguration is within the married couple, as found in the first master theme, The Power of Marriage. Indeed, all WODs under study confirmed that their marriages gave them the space and confidence to confront identity threats, as they were loved and supported by their husbands. However, the findings here appear to add to Cangià's (2018) study the dangerous consequences of having a non-understanding and non-cooperative husband, claiming that husbands' willingness to understand and empathize with their wives was the most important element of their experiences. The WODs' reflections suggest that their husbands' readiness to include them in the diplomatic process made them feel that they were part of a team who was discovering the world of diplomacy together, rather than alone, as reflected in the subtheme Togetherness.

The importance of having healthy and stable marriages in which WODs felt equal to their husbands was the only finding common to all participants, regardless of their age, employment status, countries of origin, and education levels. These findings are consistent with McNulty's (2015) study of the two main causes of divorce among expatriate couples. McNulty (2015) found that expatriate divorce mainly results from one or both of the spouses being "negatively influenced by the expatriate culture to such an extent that" one may neglect the other, or when the couple experienced core issues in their marriage prior to assignments (McNulty, 2015, p. 106).

WOD identification as part of a "team" was important for them, for it allowed them to make meaning of their presence in diplomatic postings, as shown in the master themes Making Sense of Who I Am and Who I Want to Be. Drawing upon Papanek's (1973) concept of "two-person single career," many WODs felt that they shared a purpose with their husbands, namely to make the most out of the diplomatic assignment. As a result of this inclusion, most participants perceived their presence in diplomatic assignments as important in terms of soft power, here described by Joseph Nye (1990) as the "co-optive behavioural power of getting others to do what you want through the resources of cultural attraction, ideology and international institutions" (p. 188). Many WODs took responsibility for organizing and hosting social functions, while negotiating their networks in diplomatic postings. As Domett's (2005) study on soft power has showed, WODs experienced these acts as "opportunities for exerting soft power in global politics, demonstrating how norms have important constitutive effects in shaping attitudes and therefore actions, and ultimately have material effects in shaping the processes of global politics" (p. 298).

Moreover, although unofficial, the WODs in this study felt that they were part of the performative and ritualistic aspects of diplomacy, engaging in what Constantinou (1996) described as "important global play," as shown in the sub-theme Making Sense of My Presence and sub-section I Diplomatically Matter. They perceived their roles in international diplomacy as taking place in a social environment of reciprocity and cordiality, in which key cross-cultural relationships had to be nurtured (Domett, 2005). As a result, a WOD's position as social hostess was experienced as a key activity in global diplomatic play, defined by Riordan (2003) as a process of cultural exchange characterized by social groupings and community interaction, rather than merely state-to-state negotiation. Nevertheless, although Domett's (2005) study found some differences in terms of levels of incorporation between mature and younger spouses of diplomats, the findings here show no difference across the age norm of participants. This could be because all of the participants' husbands were ambassadors, or retired ambassadors, at the time of the interviews. Domett (2005) claims that it is unclear to what extent the spouses' ages can be separated from the seniority of diplomats. Consequently, spouses of junior levels diplomats may not be as exposed to representational entertaining as spouses of senior levels diplomats, and it is yet uncertain whether their levels of involvement are triggered by any of these factors.

Interestingly, none of the WOD mentioned a desire to receive any financial remuneration for their input in diplomatic postings, suggesting perhaps that they have succumbed to the system. Another explanation would defend that receiving any form of financial salary for their unofficial work would transform the voluntary basis of their work into an official duty, removing the element of choice (Hendry, 1998).

With a more specific focus on the WOD's role enactment during diplomatic postings, the women's comments suggested that being a WOD felt quite overwhelming given their different responsibilities, as shown in the master theme My Presence is Essential. These findings resonate with the work of Davoine, et. al. (2012), which revealed the different expectations set on spouses of diplomats, namely supporting the diplomat, representing the home country, and acting as resource manager. However, the current study appears to add to these findings the struggle of managing these roles while being mothers on diplomatic assignments. The WODs' accounts, confirmed in the sub-theme Motherhood: A Two-Way Guilt, show that their biggest challenge was to balance their roles as wives and mothers, and to attend to their children's needs while being present on the diplomatic front. Their reflections suggested that feelings of guilt affected their experiences greatly, as children were at the center of many important decisions, such as moving away or staying in the home country far from the husband.

With regard to how social media may have affected WODs during diplomatic postings, this research has not found any potential psychological effect. Indeed, the only time social platforms had been mentioned throughout interviews was when all eight participants explained how social media and technology helped them feel connected to their friends and families throughout diplomatic assignments. All participants maintained that Facebook and WhatsApp helped them maintain relationships, become part of experiences through picture sharing and commenting, and belong to specific groups (Nadkarni & Hofman, 2012; Tosun, 2012), all of which were nearly impossible at earlier stages in their husbands' careers, when these technologies did not exist. A potential explanation of why social media has not affected WODs is the participants' ages. Social media as such came at a time where most participants did not feel the need to engage in upward social comparison (Vogel et al., 2014). Their self-concept was more coherent and stronger than, for example, adolescents who were in the midst of establishing their identities. Furthermore, the content which they followed social media at their specific ages was usually linked to existing interests, such as cooking, home décor, etc. Adolescents, on the other hand, were more likely to follow celebrities and role models, with the aim of resembling them (Woods & Scott, 2016).

Finally, with only three participants to draw on this study, conclusions relating to repatriation experiences must necessarily be tentative. Some WODs stated that their husbands' retirements greatly affected them, as some felt like strangers in their own home countries. They explained the difficulties in transitioning from WODs to simple wives once they came back to their home countries permanently. Similar to spouses of expatriates, this shift was for many accompanied by feelings of uncertainty, loss, and confusion, leaving WODs to undergo a similar process of adjustment to that first experienced in the diplomatic posting (Tharenou & Caulfield, 2010).

4.2.2 Theory of the Self

By using the theory of the self to frame the process of becoming a WOD, it becomes possible to see how WOD experienced and perceived diplomatic assignments as they first joined their husbands on this journey.

In his writings, Mead (1934) used the notion of game and players as an analogy for how individuals must internalize the attitudes of all members of their group in order to make meaning, have a concept of the self, and learn how to act and react. As the self has subject and object sides, the social self needs to experience itself as object, in order to see how others view the individual. This process takes place in two important ways, namely by obtaining the attitudes of all other members of the group and by organizing those in what Mead (1934) called the "generalized other."

Mead (1934) suggests that these help individuals develop their most moral, fullest, and self-conscious selves, allowing groups and communities to function according to their shared general attitudes. Although this theory was developed by understanding how children play games, Mead (1934) explained how the professional world is a simple continuation of this game for adults.

Here, WODs found themselves part of a game that they formally joined. Mead (1934) explained how each game involved a more complex form of role-playing, requiring players to internalize the roles of all other players. It is only when individuals can view themselves from the standpoint of the generalized other that self-consciousness can be fully attained. However, as these women became WODs through the process of marriage, they were expected to internalize the demands of the role, while joining a game whose rules they did not understand. The less rules are explained, the more disempowered WODs become as they are not given the right amount of information to contest the game. Moreover, to some extent, it could be argued that Foreign Services have no duty to explain the "rules of the game" to WODs, as the ministry did not employ them. As such, husbands often had to explain the rules of the game to their wives, making their interpretation of the rules crucial to WODs' understanding of the game.

In reaction to having only one source of information, many WODs explained in the sub-theme This Is Not About Me how their presence in postings could be ignored and undervalued by Foreign Services. Consequently, most of the participants expressed worries about the uncertainty of diplomatic assignments, as they did not know what was expected from these postings and what their role intended. Their failure to understand the rules translated into participants experiencing distress while attempting to make sense of their presence and purpose.

This book argues that the fundamental challenge mainly lies in their failure to understand the game. Many WODs expressed an element of choice as holding utmost importance as it helped them accept and make sense of their status as WODs. However, when thinking about the real choices presented in front of them, namely being with or without their husbands, we can understand their dilemma. Making the decision to stay with their husbands was one that did not undergo intense analysis, leading many WODs to accept the uncertainty of what awaited them, regardless of the consequences.

In light of Mead's (1934) standpoint on temporality of action and emphasis on the importance of problematic instances in human experience, this research found that what WODs experienced at this point had the utmost existential significance. An individual exists in relation to the world, and it is essential that she experiences herself in harmony with it. If this proves to be difficult or impossible, the individual is thrown in what Mead (1934) called a "crisis." Here, some WODs did experience a "crisis" in the master theme Loss of Self, as they were separated from their world and thrown into a context where loss of freedom and autonomy were first experienced (Cangià, 2018; Mead, 1934), as shown in the sub-theme Loss of Agency. Consequently, when encountering a crisis in their process of life, some WODs felt paralyzed and "stuck'" in a situation, becoming patients rather than agents of their lives.

However, many women in this study have understood through crisis that learning and internalizing the rules of the game was their only solution. Indeed, their experiences of crisis led many WODs to deepen their sense of self and to experience this realization as a turning point in their individual existences (Mead, 1934). These critical moments can be experienced negatively, with some WOD having their continuity in and with the world threatened (sub-theme: Who Am I in the New World); or positively, with WODs foreseeing opportunities to redefine, deepen, and broaden their sense of selves and the world to which they belong (sub-theme: The Need for Personal Success).

The findings here show that although crises may have destabilized WODs' sense of freedom and autonomy, they also constituted opportunities in other areas of their lives. Indeed, the discontinuities in their experiences pressured WODs to make decisions as to "what they are going to do now," leading them to find creative ways of transforming potential break-downs into break-throughs. Examples included Marta, who took up bridge; Caline and Elan, who started community schools in their postings; Sarah, who created a blog and worked intensively with refugees; and Lina, who started a charity for a children's hospital. These opportunities show how freedom denied in one aspect of experiences can be rediscovered at another level.

4.2.3 Identity Process Theory (IPT)

This book can also be located within the field of identity as the participants' struggles and obstacles throughout diplomatic assignments affected their senses of self. As a result, the findings can be linked with Breakwell's (1986, 2010) Identity Process Theory (IPT). This section will provide a framework for the integration of the personal and social aspects of WODs' identities in diplomatic postings. Indeed, keeping in mind the key identity principles of distinctiveness, self-efficacy, continuity, self-esteem (Breakwell, 1986, 1993), belonging, meaning (Vignoles et al.,

2006; Vignoles et al., 2011), and psychological coherence (Jaspal & Cinnirella, 2010), IPT sheds light on the processes that women experience as WOD. As such, I will first consider how the status of WODs during postings threatened their senses of self, and will then discuss the different coping strategies they employed in order to alleviate these identity threats.

An important moment when WODs experienced a threat to their identity was illustrated at the time diplomats received information about their first diplomatic posting as a married couple. At this moment, changes took place, as many WODs had to resign from their professions, leaving behind years of career-building. This first change of status seemed to have threatened their professional identities through all key principles of IPT, as shown in the sub-theme Wasted Intellectual Potential. Indeed, valued role identities are linked to a sense of esteem and efficacy (Ervin & Stryker, 2001) as the association of oneself with a profession is an important source of pride, confidence, and well-being (Caza & Creary, 2016). As such, professional identification played an important role on the personal level, and losing it resulted in great confusion in terms of purpose and meaning (Cangià, 2018). Many WODs expressed a fear of being intellectually empty. Others referred to their resignation process as a loss of their social environment and their sense of self, as they became different from their surroundings. While distinctiveness is generally considered a requirement for a positive sense of self, Jaspal and Cinnirella (2010) explained that when this uniqueness is predominantly negatively evaluated, here by the lack of belonging to a certain group of people, it can result in threatened identity and self-esteem.

These threats are further experienced when diplomats and their spouses arrived in their first postings and WODs experienced, through boredom mainly, a void in their professional identities. These findings can be linked to Jaspal and Cinnirella's (2010) principle of psychological coherence, an identity motive that established feelings of compatibility among individuals' interconnected identities. Their state of transition and fluidity of identity frightened many, as they were unable to recognize themselves as WODs on postings, again shown in the sub-theme Loss of Self. To a certain extent, this study established a strong link between the processes of identity and the sense of self, as for many participants the more time they spent reflecting about their lives' purposes, the more they felt disoriented, uncertain, hopeless, and frustrated about their futures.

This observation echoes Cangià's (2018) study, which revealed that the decision to embark on these diplomatic journeys had several implications on how WODs perceived themselves, especially those who made substantial investments in their educations and career development. Her findings also resonate with the WODs in this study, given that unemployment and the decision to stop working in order to accompany husbands translated into a sense of feeling powerless -- a transition from a stable working life to a transient unemployed life. This powerlessness was also characterized by WODs' transitions from financial independence to financial dependence, having both their continuity and self-efficacy removed from them.

Breakwell (1986, 2014) explained that individuals should manage threats to their identities by putting in place intra-psychic, interpersonal, and intergroup coping strategies, which our WODs evidently did (sub theme: Making Sense of My Presence). Breakwell (1986) discussed the range of coping strategies by categorizing them as either deflecting or accepting. In this study, many WODs experienced strategies of deflection during their first diplomatic assignment, as they tried to avoid or deny the existence of these threats. They rejected the idea that they were "just wives" and experienced great discomfort in social situations when having to refer to themselves as "the wife of" instead of their own names or professions.

These coping strategies negatively affected their marriages as they confronted and blamed the sources of these threats, namely their husbands, which Rosenbusch and Cseh (2012) described as the trigger for marital problems. Indeed, these deflecting strategies were associated with statements of blame, according to which WODs viewed their presence in assignments as self-sacrifice, leading them to withdraw psychologically from their presence from postings (Berry, 2003). As a result, many WODs understood that a change of coping strategy needed to take place if they wanted to save their marriages, as maintaining strategies of deflection obstructed and hindered their adjustment processes in host countries (Shaffer & Harrison, 1998) and created marital conflicts (Rosenbusch & Cseh, 2012).

Many WODs thus experienced what Breakwell (1986, 1993) called a re-evaluation of the principles of identity change, and understood that "strategies [should] be used to cope with threats and that once acceptance and changes to identity are made, a threat will fade away" (Breakwell, 1986, p. 96). The relevance of identity change with regard to expatriate spouse adjustment was first emphasized by Shaffer and Harrison (1998), who found that the experiences of expatriate spouses was oriented "strongly towards a loss and then a reclarification or reestablishment of identity" (p. 250).

This book confirmed the nature of WODs' attempts to prioritize more positive identity components and/or redefine key identity concepts. Indeed, some WODs prioritized their roles as full-time mothers, while socially implicated WODs committed strongly to their husbands. Others redefined their role and presence in diplomatic assignments by replacing their professional identities with personal projects, such as writing books or joining clubs. Participants experienced a sense of either striving or thriving across postings, with both factors serving the same purpose in giving their lives meaning. This sense of meaningfulness became a channel to accept their status as WODs, which helped them develop new aspects of their identities. The findings here provide evidence that resisting change and trying to maintain existing identities in the face of change can damage a WOD's psychological well-being and negatively impact the rest of the family.

Breakwell (1986) explained how the reconstruction and reframing of certain facets of one's experience when identity is under threatened is a common way of managing its effect. However, some participants here struggled to reconstruct their identities as many moved back and forth across the boundaries (Howard, 2000) of different identities given that they eventually went back to their previous roles and ways of life once repatriating. Indeed, given the nature of diplomatic assignments, many diplomatic families return to their home countries for approximately two years between postings, resulting in WODs' ability to work again during these repatriation periods. However, the findings of this study showed how difficult it was for them to go back to their old lives, as employers were reluctant to hire them on a temporary basis. As a result, many expressed the great difficulties of repatriation, explaining that going from one assignment to the next would be an easier process than to deal with a new set of different adjustment layers.

Studies focusing on identity construction among expatriates have provided some evidence of a range of adjustment strategies, focusing mainly on the cultural adjustment of this population (Kohonen, 2008; van Bochove & Engbersen, 2015). However, the findings here show that cultural adjustment was not an important issue for WODs, for two reasons. First, WODs must maintain a strong sense of national identity given their status of WODs. Although unofficial, they represent their countries abroad and are expected to practice their customs even abroad, guarding their sense of national identity against threats. Domett (2005) justified this strong identification as a "desire for identity, caused by perpetually moving countries, which tends to heighten nationalistic feelings towards one's home country" (p. 299). Second, the short period of time spent in each host country does not provide the time and space for WODs to adopt acculturation strategies (Berry, 2003) and replace their own national identities with the host countries', as opposed to immigration or single long-term expatriation assignment.

Some threats of national identity obtained among WODs who married diplomats of different nationalities. Within this research project, both Marta and Ava married men from different countries and explained having to let go of their own nationalities in order to make place for a new one. As suggested by Breakwell and Lyons (1996), principles of IPT, which are applied to personal identities, can also be applied to social identities such as WODs' national identities.

4.3 Strengths, Limitations and Transferability

In order to consider the transferability of this study, I will revisit issues of research quality and consider its limitations by reflecting on the methodological, procedural, personal, and epistemological challenges I faced. This section will end with a clear statement of transferability.

4.3.1 Methodological Reflexivity

This book aimed at following the principles for "good practice" (Elliott, Fischer & Rennie, 1999) while conducting qualitative research. Some of these principles can be conceptualized as usefulness, rigor, and quality of the research, and have been addressed in the Methodology Chapter. A number of additional criteria should be considered in this section.

Qualitative research has been accused of lacking scientific rigor (Silverman, 2013) with some criticizing it for lacking generalizability, objectivity, and reproducibility (Evans, 2017; Krahn & Putnam, 2003). Concepts of validity and reliability are understood differently in qualitative research, and some researchers claim that in cases of qualitative research reliability should be grounded in the context of the epistemological position that the research project undertakes (Madill, Jordan & Shirley, 2000). In this case, the epistemological position (see Section 2.4) implies that there is no attempt whatsoever to reach reliability in the positivistic way, as one can argue that objectivity is a myth and that any efforts to be impartial to any research will fail (Flick, 2009).

My epistemological position argues that "diverse perspectives can provide a fuller understanding of social psychological phenomena" (Madill et al., 2000, p. 17), and that it is therefore better for researchers to be transparent and upfront about their subjectivities and assumptions, allowing readers to draw their own conclusions about any interpretations made (Austin & Sutton, 2014). Also, Madill, et. al. (2000) explain that it is important to state clearly the epistemological position the researcher takes and to conduct the study in an epistemologically consistent way. Hence, I tried to channel my epistemological stance in the second chapter, as well as demonstrating transparency about my relationship with the data and by grounding the findings in WODs' personal accounts, as suggested by Yardley (2008).

Although I followed all four of Yardley's (2008) principles carefully, I do not claim that the findings are the only credible accounts that could have emerged from these interviews (Smith, et. al., 2009). I recognize that there are alternative interpretations of the same data, and that another researcher could reach different conclusions. I also recognize that another researcher could have generated different data from the interviews, and that if WODs were interviewed at a different time or on a different day, different meanings and understandings of their experiences might have emerged. Consequently, this research project solely claims to report the understandings and experiences of these eight WODs, although it maintains and believes that the findings presented above are novel, important, potentially relevant to other women, and some men, who share salient characteristics with these WODs.

With specific regard to IPA, my reasons for using this approach were discussed in the Methodology chapter (see section 2.5); however, its use in this study is not without limitations (Brocki & Wearden, 2006). Some researchers have criticized IPA for its dependency on the validity of language, that is, requiring participants to be highly articulate and able to communicate clearly the meaning they make of their experiences (Willig,

2008, 2013). As a result, extensive attention has been paid to the role discourse and language played in shaping WODs' experiences and understanding the phenomena under investigation. Furthermore, in her book, Willig (2013) argues the suitability of participants' accounts by suggesting that IPA should only be used when participants can adequately and sophistically articulate the "rich texture of their experiences" (p. 67). All of the participants in this study were motivated to talk about their experiences, as they were self-selected, and most had at least an undergraduate degree. Also, although all participants had English as their second or third language, they were all fluent and were able to articulate and communicate their perceptions, feelings, and thoughts in words. I acknowledge that the decision to conduct the interviews in a language other than their mother tongues could have limited their ability to express themselves freely and fully. However, the material that emerged was still significant.

Keeping in mind that my main aim was to allow WODs individual voices through this approach, I decided to put emphasis on the kind of communication they used, rather than to ignore some aspects of it. Within the analysis, careful attention was given to how they communicated their meaning-making and focused extensively on the expressions and metaphors they used, which has brought many interesting insights about the phenomenon. Additionally, as IPA has been criticized for over-focusing on cognition (Willig, 2012) with a focus on meanings, processes, and thoughts, IPA researchers acknowledge that embodiment of the phenomenon can be as important (Smith et al., 2009). Hence, careful attention was given to any type of embodied expressions, feelings, and non-verbal communication, leading the analysis to focus not only on "deliberate, controlled reflections" (Smith et al., 2009, p. 189), but also on pre-reflective experiences. As a result, there were moments during interviews when I highlighted these non-verbal cues and aimed to elaborate on them. However, I felt that some participants were not comfortable with this approach, as they seemed to feel challenged by my detections of different meanings. Consequently, I decided to not voice these non-verbal cues and instead annotated them in my interview journal once the interview ended, resulting in what I hope a richer analysis of the data.

4.3.2 Procedural Reflexivity

Participants were selected in the order in which they replied to my e-mails, removing concerns about researcher bias. Two WODs agreed to take part in the study, but withdraw their participation before the interview, stating that they did not feel mentally prepared to discuss their experiences. These two WODs attracted my attention further, for I speculated that the diplomatic lifestyle may have been the reason for their unreadiness to share their experiences. The little contact I had with these WODs affected my initial assumptions about this population in general, leading me to think that this lifestyle had negatively affected them. In reflection, I had to remind myself that many reasons, diplomatic or not, could be at the center of their decisions, and that it was my ethical responsibility to not interpret them.

While the sample was homogenous in terms of women all married to diplomats, it was heterogeneous in terms of age, husband's employment status, sociocultural backgrounds, and place of residence. Such heterogeneity added to the diverse experiences of being a WOD, but also ran the risk of complicating the data. Given that each country has its own laws and agreements on spousal rights, some important variation resulted in different experiences in terms of quality of life. However, despite their countries of origin, all WODs shared common experiences, with only relatively minor variations.

Upon reflection, I feel that any additional depth or width of analysis that may have arisen when choosing a more homogeneous sample would have been offset because there was no research data to support choosing a more homogeneous sample. I feel that the novelty of this particular topic in the psychological field was a rational reason to choose a heterogeneous sample and a good starting point for further research on the topic. Notably, the relatively heterogeneous nature of the sample may have benefitted the extent of transferability of the findings to other women who share key features of the participants, such as multiple relocations and military wives (Storms, 2014), international executives' wives (Hochschild, 2005), single-career couples, and politicians' wives (Gill & Haurin, 1998; Rifkind, 2000; Todd, 1995). I do believe, however, that this sample is unique, and that few wives share all common characteristics.

In regards to the interview process, I was acutely aware of the potentially different power dynamics. I remained mindful of how participants may experience my position as a researcher and how their political status might effect me. At the beginning of every interview, I felt slightly intimidated by the formality of the encounter, as I traveled to their diplomatic or private residences, interacted with staff members, and even sometimes met the diplomat spouse himself. I paid close attention to remaining professional and to avoid coming across as intrusive or invading the diplomat and his family's privacy. On the other hand, I was keen to give the WODs the space they needed in order to feel comfortable to share their experiences and be non-judgmentally heard. In an attempt to put off the pressure, participants and I engaged in small talks prior to interviews, in which they would ask me questions about my interest in the topic or about our mutual contact. Before starting the interview, I also made it a point to remind the WODs of their rights of confidentiality and option to decline to answer any question.

After each interview, I made the decision to turn off the audio-recorder, as all WODs expressed an interest in engaging in off the record conversations. During these informal conversations, many WODs shared difficult moments they had experienced with their husbands and/or children. Some of their revelations accentuated the difficulty in talking about these issues when any formalities were taking place (in this case, the audio-recorder). Consequently, I consider this to be one of the limitations of using solely semi-structured interviews with this specific population, as they could have been regarded mostly as another formal encounter. In the future, I would consider additional forms of data-gathering that would enhance trustworthiness, such as diaries or multiple interviews at different points in time.

In conducting the interviews, I found myself allowing for different data to come up for participants. Indeed, initial interviews were long (my first interview lasted three hours) as a result of my openness and urge to give participants the space they needed. This translated into a significant amount of data to analyze and, given my commitment to being thorough and rigorous in my analysis (Yardley, 2008), it became exceptionally time-consuming and stressful. Over time, I believe I became better at managing the balance between giving WODs space to talk about certain topics and focusing on the interview schedule and the flow I had set up. Although this resulted in a great amount of data to transcribe and analyze, I believe that my attempts to empower these women were well received, which may have allowed them to open up further during our informal conversations. Surprisingly, I thought that my status of trainee was going to challenge me into wanting to fall more into "therapist mode." However, I found myself knowing where the limit was set and being congruent with my role as a research interviewer, rather than as a trainee.

4.3.3 Personal and Epistemological Reflexivity

Being a trainee has unsurprisingly affected some choices in regards to the research study. My choice of IPA, for instance, sat well with the ethos of counseling psychology and the kind of focus it puts on participants. Reflecting on this study's epistemological standpoint, I realize that as WODs described contradictions and/or directions of the same experience, the project itself also held some epistemological tensions. These tensions mainly resided between (1) a need to stay as close as possible to the participants' experiences while providing definitions, theoretical explanations, and meaning-making; (2) analyzing the data by finding the right balance between describing and interpreting the participants' experiences; and (3) being curious and giving a voice to a minority, while staying as open and neutral as possible. Larkin, Watts, and Clifton (2006) also highlight these tensions in IPA by explaining how attentive the researcher needs to be when describing and interpreting the phenomenon in question, while acknowledging the role of the participants and researchers.

Although the first two tensions mentioned above have always been on my mind, it is the third tension that I mostly struggled with, hence influencing the first two. Indeed, reflecting back on the research process,

I am aware that I was in some sense moving back and forth between my initial interest in the topic based on anecdotes, and the [lack of] theoretical evidence in regards to the phenomenon. Since the beginning, this topic triggered a sense of injustice I was seeing among WOD. In fact, at the beginning of this project I realized how close-minded and one-sided my perception of the phenomenon was. I had absorbed anecdotal accounts and concluded what I thought at the time was the only possible experience of being a WOD.

I soon understood that my investigation was doomed to fail if a serious change of perspective did not occur. As a result, my personal experiences and involvement in the research took a serious turn when I became aware of my assumptions. My first interview schedule draft revealed clear epistemological incongruency, as many of my questions alluded to my personal assumptions about WODs. With the help of my supervisor, I quickly understood that I needed to distance myself from my assumptions and realize that I did not know anything of the phenomenon in question. Consequently, I actively sought to remain mindful of this pitfall throughout the data collection, analysis, and write-up processes, and kept beside me a reflective diary throughout the process to ensure a proper balance between what is said in the data and was is based on my assumptions. Additionally, the inclusion of the first and final draft of my interview schedule in this research felt important, as I wanted to show the readers transparency in my development as a researcher.

Additionally, I spent time reading examples of other IPA studies in order to familiarize myself with the necessary mixture of description and interpretation in analyzing the data. Nonetheless, as a novice researcher, I found myself sometimes lacking the courage to formulate an interpretation and sought refuge in a middle ground that I could follow more passively. Upon reflection, I realized that my fear in interpreting the findings stemmed from my apprehension in appearing somewhat assumptive of WODs' experiences. It was at this point that I understood how bracketing was not always possible, but rather that an awareness and reexamination of my pre-existing beliefs and a re-examination was necessary (Halling, Leifer & Rowe, 2006).

A helpful way to find this balance came by presenting a TEDx Talk on WODs and preparing a PowerPoint presentation for the annual conference of the European Union of Foreign Affairs Spouses Association (EUFASA). As I was preparing these presentations, I was reminded of the WODs who listened to my content and agreed or disagreed to with it. Consequently, I carefully considered my interpretations, as I did not want to impose any unwarranted conclusions about their experiences.

This has been a burden that I carried throughout my research, as I knew that my findings were telling only one side of the story. Indeed, during my presentation for the EUFASA conference, I quickly realized that my findings could vary completely depending on the nationality of the WODs, as every diplomatic service has its own rules and requirements. As such, I became more aware of the multitudes of different experiences WODs could have, and aimed at being sensitive to them by acknowledging that my findings may or may not resonate with some spouses of diplomats. Moreover, I have paid great attention to the way I interpreted my findings and always found myself asking the question, "What would my participants think of this sentence if they were to read this project?"

On a more personal level, I feel that during the process of this research I myself experienced some of the uncertainties that I discuss throughout the study. As an international student, my time in the United Kingdom was coming to an end, and the next steps for my future are soon to be decided. Although a part of me felt the need to go back to my home country and establish a professional identity there, I found myself in a position similar to that of my participants, as my fiancé may need to remain or relocate to a country different from our home country. All these uncertainties and transitions brought me to reevaluate some of my identity components by asking myself questions such as "Who do I want to be?" These personal experiences, together with the experiences of the many spouses of diplomats I have met, had a discernible effect on me in that it strengthened my passion for social justice, community psychology, and feminism. While I have had comparatively little exposure to the outside world, I remain very excited to see how my passion for raising awareness about prejudices and injustices will shape my own future.

4.3.4 Conclusion

Although this study has limitations and only pretends to report one version of findings on the experiences and understandings of eight WODs, its novel themes and significant insights have noteworthy implications, relevance, and transferability to others, men and women, who share salient characteristics with the participants.

4.4 Relevance to Counseling Psychology and Implications for Practice

This book sheds light on a population that is little researched, rarely seeks help, often fears judgments, and can feel socially isolated. Consequently, this study may be a useful source for mental health professionals, including counseling psychologists and other practitioners, who work with clients experiencing difficulties with expatriation.

One consequence that mental practitioners should keep in mind when working with women in similar contexts is the multiple levels of identity threats experienced in expatriation and repatriation. They should explore in great depth the meanings held for each identity component, while paying careful attention to how their sociocultural and personal contexts may influence their experiences. They should also reflect on the range of coping strategies used to deflect or accept (Breakwell,1986) a new situation and to explore the impact these may have on their well-being.

All of the participants who took part in this study expressed gratification in speaking about their experiences, with some even mentioning that it was the first time that the attention was on them instead of their husbands. Several shared that the interviews were a rewarding process, suggesting that it felt good to reflect on the many years spent serving their countries alongside their husbands, while gaining a new perspective and understanding of their experiences.

These comments disclosed how valuable and important it is to talk about one's experiences, as many WODs reflected on the therapeutic benefits of doing so. In fact, during our off-the-record conversations, some WODs revealed that they had relied on anti-depressants and/or alcohol because they did not have anybody to talk to while being on postings. They explained that language barriers, the relatively short amount of time spent in host countries, and fears of being judged made it difficult for them to seek therapeutic help, but that they also saw potential benefits of it. As a result, counseling psychologists should be encouraged to understand the importance of letting clients talk as freely and openly as possible about their understanding of their experiences (Harrist, 2006), as doing so outside the therapy room can feel relatively threatening.

The diversity of WODs' experiences emphasized the importance of assuming a "not-knowing" and curious stance. By admitting that stereotypical social representations of diplomats and their lifestyles as "glamorous" can be misleading, therapists should be aware that these assumptions may reflect their own perceptions. As with any client entering therapeutic space, mental health practitioners have a responsibility to reflect on their biases and not impose them on their clients.

Almost all participants described not knowing what to expect from their new journey left them feeling insecure about their futures. Many experienced a sense of uncertainty about their roles and professional identities before, during, and after diplomatic assignments. Elan, for example, discussed attending diplomatic training. She explained that these were helpful for imparting practical knowledge of what to expect from postings and what her role was intended to be. Nevertheless, she expressed regret that the training failed to address mental health issues that spouses were to face, with many WODs resorting to personal contacts in order to anticipate what their life was going to be like. Consequently, it seems important when working with women who are accompanying their spouses to reflect on their understandings of being a WOD, to consider their hopes and expectations, and to reflect on the different challenges that might impede them. This can be an opportunity for counseling psychologists to join address these issues through individual or group sessions.

Additionally, this study calls for family and couples therapists to pay careful attention to issues of control and agency for expatriate spouses, especially the ones who may lose their professional identities in the process and become financially dependent on their spouses. Hence, therapists should focus on the shift in the relationship dynamic in order to help couples and families make sense of these changes, especially since the health of marriages has been found to be one of the leading factors in the quality of diplomatic performance (McNulty, 2015).

With so much attention placed on diplomats, very little is directed to their spouses, which, in light of this study, seems vital. Therapists should be encouraged to help spouses think about what happens to them once they are on diplomatic postings. Many diplomatic services simply ignore the presence of spouses or take their presence for granted, leaving them feeling disempowered while still expecting her to make sense of who she is without any support. It therefore seems to be an ethical responsibility for diplomatic services to provide the necessary support to help accompanying spouses make sense of their transitions and to raise awareness about the conflicting issues they may experience. Undeniably, developing awareness can significantly improve WODs' psychological well-being and help them reach a certain sense of accepting their new situations by promoting therapeutic change in their perception and understanding (Greenberg & Watson, 2006; Robbins & Jolkovski, 1987).

It may be relevant for counseling psychologists to share some of the obstacles WODs experience, especially if they are struggling to foresee potential threats. In line with Breakwell's (1986) work, therapists should encourage and invite their clients to consider how they might manage extant or potential threats and difficulties. They may also keep in mind that many WODs may well be excited and grateful for the opportunity to be posted abroad. Nonetheless, therapists should take the opportunity to introduce some of the meanings, assumptions, stereotypes, and connotations associated with the labels of being an accompanying spouse (also sometimes referred to as "trailing spouse"), inviting clients to reevaluate these issues in order to accept their novel and ambivalent identities.

One way to do so is by following Harrist's (2006) claim that the best way to manage ambivalence and confusion is to develop a greater sense of awareness and flexibility in the ways in which this uncertainty is experienced and addressed. Patients are to be encouraged to develop a sense of acceptance and appreciation for the complexity of their situations, emotions, and meanings (e.g. seeing them as adventures, or chances of spending more time with their children), and use them as opportunities for growth rather than potential regressions. By facilitating this process and educating clients on how becoming a WOD might affect them, therapists engage, to a certain degree, in what Miller (1969) terms "give Psychology away." By "giving Psychology away," mental health professionals offer patients a better perception and understanding of who they are, the choices they have, and who they can be -- all inquiries that can lead them to exercise further control over their own lives (Banyard & Hulme, 2015). Although one could argue that these are patriarchal solutions, it is important to remember that WODs do still live in a patriarchal society where choices of management are limited.

Consequently, this research aims to combat patriarchal norms by providing WODs more support and protection. Indeed, while it may seem grandiose to suggest this outcome given this research project's relatively small scale there appears to be a need to promote the establishment of family offices in diplomatic services that would be entirely dedicated to diplomatic spouses and their families. Many European countries have already seen the advantages of such institutions (European Union of Foreign Affairs Spouses Association, 2018) and recommend their creation not only to acknowledge a family's presence in diplomatic postings, but also to recognize their importance in them. These institutions could use psychological knowledge formed from the effect of being an accompanying spouse of a diplomat and petition for new laws and rights that would protect and support spouses, such as individual allowances, divorce procedures, and pension rights. Additionally, this study's findings suggest the value of implementing further bilateral agreements between countries would allow accompanying spouses to work. By allowing WODs to have professional identities, some existing tensions could easily be relieved.

In his antidotes for arrogance, Kelly (1970) claimed that psychologists should broaden their definition of therapy, expand their criteria for what makes a competent helper, become participants in their community, and change their time perspectives in order to help build "a psychology of the community" (p. 524). His redefinition of the psychologist's role calls for a deeper exploration of the responsibilities of counseling psychologists, with Fassinger and Morrow (2013) and Rafalin (2010) explaining that they have a duty to advocate for social justice. This study according aims to help promote "equity and equality for individuals in society in terms of access to a number of different resources and opportunities, the right to self-determination, and a balancing of power across society" (Cutts, 2013, p. 8).

The British Psychological Society (2017) expects accredited counseling psychologists to "effectively communicate clinical and nonclinical information from a psychological perspective in a style appropriate to a variety of different audiences" (p. 15). They are encouraged to communicate these issues and inspire the responsible parties to dedicate a part of their resources to accompanying spouses. Such support can take the form of trainings for diplomats and their spouses, both in groups and individually. Their aim would be to increase awareness of the difficulties that they may encounter as their identities shift, and the different ways research, rather than anecdotes, suggests they could manage these difficulties and transitions.

Practical training, such as language courses and protocol guidance, would also help accompanying spouses acclimate to each new host country. Furthermore, the experiences under study here suggest that such training should focus on providing appropriate support to WODs who are mothers in order to minimize the struggles that are associated to it. Such support could take the form of "ready-packages," in which spouses could find all the relevant information, such as medical referrals and schools with international programs.

As a final point, this research project has implications for future psychological research and scholarships. Counseling psychology has tended to ignore diplomatic wives because they seem powerful and privileged compared to other social groups. This study's findings, however, may allow psychologists and other professionals to be more sensitive and aware of their own assumptions and biases with regard to different minorities.

4.5 Areas for Future Research

In light of the significant gap of literature on the experiences of WODs who accompany their spouses on diplomatic postings, this study may serve as a preliminary starting point for further research. Given the sample's size and heterogeneity, the next step might logically be to conduct similar research on a larger and/or more homogeneous sample of WODs who represent the same country abroad. Because each country differs in its own laws and customs, it would be worth looking at how they shape the experiences of accompanying diplomats to see whether a phenomenological exploration of their experiences would yield similar perceptions and understandings of the phenomenon.

A study that explores how each law and right granted to spouses of diplomats affect their experiences as accompanying spouse would provide greater understandings and a fuller picture of how WODs experience themselves. More specifically, given that Estonia is the only country to provide a monthly stipend of €1,000 to accompanying spouses (EUFASA, 2018), it may be valuable to study the effect that this financial incentive has on WODs' experiences.

It may be of additional value to examine the experiences of ex-wives of diplomats who divorced or separated from their husbands during diplomatic assignments. Considering the important role of marriage in shaping and defining WOD experiences, it feels natural to ask how this experience changes when WODs and diplomats themselves no longer feel supported in their marriages.

In light of the increasing diversity of professional diplomats, further research from a phenomenological point of view might productively focus on the husbands of female diplomats (HODs?), unmarried partners, and same-sex spouses/partners. Considering the effect of gender identity on accompanying a diplomat will provide insight into a new wave of roles and expectations.

Given this research's interest in transferability, it would be helpful to conduct comparative research between different groups that share common experiences with WOD, such as military spouses. Such studies could help identify the particular and unique experiences of WODs, while investigating the similarities within both groups.

Another potential area of research that emerged from this study was the effect of diplomatic life on children. Some participants indeed wondered if that lifestyle had negatively or positively affected their children. Their curiosity may have stemmed from the guilt many felt with regard to their children, and my inability to answer their questions served as reassurance. Researching children of diplomats in their own right may well be an important subject of its own.

In relation to therapeutic practice, since very little research has addressed how WODs might manage identity threats focusing on clients who lack agency and control could be highly beneficial.

Lastly, most of the accounts of diplomatic families and their struggles with mental health have been anecdotal, rather than scientific. Attempting to understand the psychological consequences of frequent mobility and the condition of mental health in diplomatic families deserves inquiry.

4.6 Conclusion

This book has tried to advance our understanding of WODs' experiences across diplomatic assignments. It attempted to show how a qualitative exploration of this group might provide valuable insights into the exploration of meaning and identity processes in the world of diplomatic spouses, the "real housewives of diplomacy." Its findings have significant implications not only for the accompanying spouses themselves, but also for the operation of national diplomatic services and the field of counseling psychology.

Following Domett's (2005) contention that diplomatic spouses have always exerted soft power in public diplomacy, this study believes that spouses can be made invisible by gendered ideologies, structures, and power, which in some circumstances kept them in the background for a very long time (Davoine, et. al., 2013). It is from this ideology that I took interest in giving these spouses a voice to share their experiences in a framework that I hope will be relevant and informative.

Having recently completed my doctoral training, I wrote this book to counter Agaoglu's (2013) claim that doctorate candidates leave their research to "simply sit on the shelf at the university gathering dust" (p. 1). In fact, my passion for this topic has only increased, and my intention to include further study in my professional mission is one that I take seriously. I hope to explore the different facets of this phenomenon and to help spouses of diplomats in general live fuller lives. In fulfillment of this goal, I hope always to be able to look at myself in the mirror and say that I am proud of what I see, and to continue my work.

References

Aalbers, G., McNally, R. J., Heeren, A., de Wit, S., & Fried, E. I. (2018). Social media and depression symptoms: A network perspective. *Journal of Experimental Psychology: General*.

Adler, N. (1986), *International dimensions of organizational behavior*, Kent Publishing, Boston, MA.

Adler, N.J. and Gundersen, A. (2008), *International dimensions of organizational behaviour*, 5th ed., Cengage Learning, Mason, OH.

Agaoglu, A. (2013). *Why No 'Me' in PhD?* [Blog Post]. Retrieved from: https://www.theguardian.com/higher-education network/blog/2013/apr/19/academicwriting-first-person-singular

Andreason, A. (2008). Expatriate adjustment of spouses and expatriate managers: An integrative research review, *International Journal of Management, 25(2)*, pp. 382-395.

Appadurai, A. (1990). Disjuncture and difference in the global cultural economy. *Theory, Culture and Society*, 7, 295–310.

Appel, H., Gerlach, A. L., & Crusius, J. (2016). The interplay between Facebook use, social comparison, envy, and depression. *Current Opinion in Psychology*, *9*, 44–49.

Arieli, D. (2007). The task of being content: Expatriate wives in Beijing, emotional work and patriarchal bargain. *Journal of International Women's Studies*, *8*(4), 18-31.

Austin, Z., & Sutton, J. (2014). Qualitative Research: Getting Started. *Canadian Journal of Hospital Pharmacy, 67*(6), 436-440.

Aycan, Z. and Kanungo, R.N. (1997), "Current issues and future challenges in expatriation research", in Saunders, D.M. and Aycan, Z. (Eds), *New Approaches to Employee Management*, JAI Press, Greenwich, CT, pp. 245-260.

Banyard, P. & Hulme, J. A. (2015). Giving psychology away: How George Miller's vision is being realized by psychological literacy. *Psychology Teaching Review, 21*(2), 93-101.

Bausinger, H. (1999). "Intercultural demands and cultural identity". In T. Vestergaard, (Ed.), *Language, Culture and Identity* (pp. 259-282). Aalborg, Denmark: Aalborg University Press.

Beaverstock, J. V. (2002). Transnational elites in global cities: British expatriates in Singapore's financial district. *Geoforum* 33 (4): 525–38.

Beers, W. (1992). *Women and sacrifice: Male narcissism and the psychology of religion*. Detroit, MI: Wayne State University Press.

Berger, U., Keshet, H., & Gilboa-Schechtman, E. (2017). Self-evaluations in social anxiety: The combined role of explicit and implicit social-rank. *Personality and Individual Differences, 104*, 368–373.

Berry, J.W. (2003). Conceptual approaches to acculturation. In K. Chun, P. Balls Organista & G. Marin (Eds), *Acculturation: Advances in Theory, Measurement and Applied Research* (pp. 17–37). Washington, DC: American Psychological Association.

Bhaskar-Shrinivas, P., Harrison, D.A., Shaffer, M.A. and Luk, D.M. (2005), Input-based and time-based models of international adjustment: Meta-analytic evidence and theoretical extensions, *Academy of Management Journal*, 48(2), 257-281.

Bielby, W. T., & Bielby, D. D. (1992). I will follow him: Family ties, gender-role beliefs, and reluctance to relocate for a better job. *American Journal Of Sociology, 97*(5), 1241-1267.

Black, A. (2001) "Ambiguity and verbal disguise within diplomatic culture", In Hendrey, J. and Watson, C.W.(eds.) *An anthropology of indirect communication*. London: Routledge, pp. 255-270.

Black, J.S., Mendenhall, M.E. and Oddou, G. (1991), Toward a comprehensive model of international adjustment: An integration of multiple theoretical perspectives, *Academy of Management Review*, 16(2), 291-317.

Black, J. and Stephens, G. (1989), The influence of the spouse on American expatriate adjustment and intent to stay in pacific rim overseas assignments, *Journal of Management*, 15(4), 529-544.

Breakwell, G. M. (1983). Formulations and searches. In G. M. Breakwell (Ed.), *Threatened Identities* (pp. 3-26). New York: John Wiley & Sons.

Breakwell, G. M. (1986). *Coping with threatened identities.* London: Methuen.

Breakwell, G. M. (1992). Introduction. In G. M. Breakwell (Ed.), *Social Psychology of Identity and the Self Concept* (pp. 1-8). London: Surrey University Press.

Breakwell, G. M. (2010). Resisting representations and identity processes. *Papers on Social Representations, 19,* 6.1-6.11.

Breakwell, G. M. (2014). Identity Process Theory: Clarifications and elaborations. In R. Jaspal & G. M. Breakwell (Eds.), *Identity Process Theory: Identity, social action and social change* (pp. 23). Cambridge, England: Cambridge University Press.

Breakwell, G. M., & Lyons, E. (1996). *Changing European identities. Social psychological analysis of social change.* Oxford, England: Butterworth- Heinemann.

Brewer, M. B., & Gardner, W. (1996). Who is this "we"? Levels of collective identity and self representations. *Journal of Personality and Social Psychology, 71(1),* 83-93.

British Psychological Society (2017) *Standards for the Accreditation of Doctoral Programmes in Counseling Psychology.* Leicester: BPS

Brocki, J. M., & Wearden, A. J. (2006). A critical evaluation of the use of interpretative phenomenological analysis (IPA) in health psychology. *Psychology and Health, 21*(1), 87-108.

Bunge, M. (1993). Realism and antirealism in social science. *Theory and Decision,* 35(3), 207-235.

Burns, R. B. (2000). *Introduction to research methods.* SAGE publications. *United States of America.*

Byrne, M. M. (2001). Understanding life experiences through a phenomenological approach to research. *Association of Operating Room Nurses. AORN Journal, 73*(4), 830.

Callan, H. (1975). *"The premise of dedication: Notes toward an ethnography of diplomats' wives."* Pp. 87-104 in Shirley Ardener (ed.), Perceiving Women. New York: Halsted Press.

Callan, H. & Ardener, S., (1984). *The incorporated wife.* London: Croom Helm.

Cangià, F. (2018). Precarity, imagination, and the mobile life of the 'Trailing spouse'. *Ethos*, 46(1), 8-26.

Cangià, F., & Zittoun, T. (2018). EDITORIAL: When "expatriation" is a matter of family. opportunities, barriers and intimacies in international mobility. *Migration Letters*, 15(1), 1-16.

Carter, M. & Grover, V. (2015). Me, My Self, and I(T): Conceptualizing information technology identity and its implications. *Mis Quarterly*.

Caza, B. B., and Creary S.J. (2016). The construction of professional identity. In A. Wilkinson, D. Hislop, and C. Coupland (eds.), *Perspectives on Contemporary Professional Work: Challenges and Experiences*: 259–285. Cheltenham, UK: Elgar.

Chen, A., Lu, Y., Chau, P.Y.K. & Gupta, S. (2014). Classifying, measuring, and predicting users' overall active behavior on social networking sites. *Journal of Management Information Systems, 31,* 213-253.

Chiang, M. (2015). Sojourning in the margin: Living as wives of international students. *Dissertation Abstracts International Section A, 76*.

Cho, J. & Trent, A. (2006). Validity in qualitative research revisited. *Qualitative Research, 6(3),* 319-340.

Clarke, C. (2009). An introduction to interpretative phenomenological analysis: A useful approach for occupational therapy research. *British journal of occupational therapy, 72*(1), 37-39.

Clodius, J. E., & Magrath, D. S. (Eds.). (1984). *The president's spouse: Volunteer or volunteered.* Washington, DC: National Association of State Universities and Land-Grant Colleges.

Cieri, H. D., Dowling, P. J., & F. Taylor, K. (1991). The psychological impact of expatriate relocation on partners. *The International Journal of Human Resource Management, 2*(3), 377-414.

Cole, N. (2011), Managing global talent: Solving the spousal adjustment problem, *The International Journal of Human Resource Management*, 22(7)1504-1530.

Collins, H. E., & Bertone, S. (2017). Threatened identities: Adjustment narratives of expatriate spouses. *Journal of Global Mobility: The Home of Expatriate Management Research, 5*(1), 78-92.

Constantinou, C. (1996) *On the way to diplomacy*. Minneapolis, MN: University of Minnesota Press.

Cooper, M. (2009). Welcoming the Other: Actualising the humanistic ethic at the core of Counseling psychology practice. *Counseling Psychology Review, 24*(3&4), 119–129.

Côté, J. E. (2006). Identity studies: How close are we to establishing a social science of identity? An appraisal of the field. Identity: *An International Journal of Theory and Research*, 6(1), 3-25.

Coyle, A. (2007). Introduction to qualitative psychological research. In E. Lyons & A. Coyle (Eds.), *Analysing Qualitative Data in Psychology* (pp.9-30). London: Sage.

Coyle, A. & Rafalin, D. (2000). Jewish gay men's accounts of negotiating cultural, religious, and sexual identity: A qualitative study. *Journal of Psychology & Human Sexuality*, 12(4), 21-48.

Cranston, S. (2016). Producing migrant encounter: Learning to be a british expatriate in singapore through the global mobility industry. *Environment and Planning D: Society and Space, 34*(4), 655-671.

Cutts, L.A. (2013). Considering a Social Justice Agenda for Counseling Psychology in the United Kingdom. *Counseling Psychology Review, 28(2)*, 8-16.

Davis, J. E. (Ed.). (2011). *Identity and social change*. Transaction Publishers.

Davoine, E., Ravasi, C., Salamin, X., & Cudré-Mauroux, C. (2013). A "dramaturgical" analysis of spouse role enactment in expatriation: An exploratory gender comparative study in the diplomatic and consular field.*Journal of Global Mobility: The Home of Expatriate Management Research,1*(1), 92-112.

Dearnley, C. (2005). A reflection on the use semi-structured interviews. *Nurse*

Researcher, 13(1), 19-28.

De Singly, F., & Chaland, K. (2002). Avoir le " second rôle " dans une équipe conjugale: Le cas des femmes de préfet et de sous-préfet. *Revue française de sociologie*, 43(1), 127-158.

DeVito, M. A., Birnholtz, J., Hancock, J. T. (2017). Platforms, people, and perception:

Using affordances to understand self-presentation on social

media. *Proceedings of the 20th Annual ACM Conference on Computer-Supported Cooperative Work and Social Computing*, 740-754.

Deaux, K. (1993). Personalizing identity and socializing self. In G. M. Breakwell (Ed.), *Social Psychology of Identity and the Self Concept* (pp. 9-34). London: Surrey University Press.

Dhir, A., Yossatorn, Y., Kaur, P., & Chen, S. (2018). Online social media fatigue and psychological well-being: A study of compulsive use, fear of missing out, fatigue, anxiety and depression. *International Journal of Information Management, 40*, 141–152

Dilthey, W. (1976). The development of hermeneutics (H. Rickman, Trans.). In H. Rickman (Ed.), *Dilthey, selected writings* (pp. 246-263). Cambridge, England: Cambridge University Press. (Original work published 1900).

Domett, T. (2005). Soft power in global politics? Diplomatic partners as transversal actors. *Australian Journal of Political Science*, 40(2), 289-306.

Dovidio, J. F., & Esses, V. M. (2001). Immigrants and immigration: Advancing the psychological perspective. *Journal of Social Issues, 57(3),* 375-387.

Dressel, P. L. (1992). *Patriarchy and social welfare work*. In Y. Hasenfeld (Ed.), *Human services as complex organizations* (pp. 205–223). Thousand Oaks, CA: Sage.

Dryden, C. (1999). *Being married, doing gender: A critical anlysis of gender relationships in marriage*. London, England: Routledge.

Easthope, H. (2009). Fixed identities in a mobile world? The relationship between mobility, place, and identity. *Identities: Global Studies in Culture and Power*, 16, 61–82.

Eatough, V., & Smith, J. A. (2008). Interpretative phenomenological analysis. In C. Willig & W. Stainton-Rogers (Eds.), *The SAGE handbook of qualitative research in psychology* (pp. 179-194). London: SAGE Publications.

Elhai, J. D., Levine, J. C., Dvorak, R. D., & Hall, B. J. (2016). Fear of missing out, need

for touch, anxiety and depression are related to problematic smartphone use. *Computers in Human Behavior*, 63, 509–516.

Elliott, R., Fischer, C. T., & Rennie, D. L. (1999). Evolving guidelines for publication of qualitative research studies in psychology and related fields. *The British Journal of Clinical Psychology, 38*(3), 215-229.

Erickson, R. J. (2005). Why Emotion Work Matters: Sex, Gender, and the Division of Household Labor. *Journal Of Marriage And Family, 67*(2), 337-351.

Erickson, R. J., & Ritter, C. (2001). Emotional labor, burnout, and inauthenticity: Does gender matter? *Social Psychology Quarterly, 64*(2), 146-163.

Ervin, L.H. and Stryker, S. (2001). Theorizing the relationship between self-esteem and identity. In T.J. Owens and S. Stryker (eds), *Extending Self-Esteem Theory and Research: Sociological and Psychological Currents.* New York: Cambridge University Press, pp. 29-55.

European Union Foreign Affairs Spouses, Partners and Families Association (2018), available at: www.eufasa.org (accessed May 05, 2018).

Evans, M. (2017). Reliability and Validity in Qualitative Research by Teacher Researchers. In E. Wilson (Ed.), *School-based Research: A Guide for Education Students* (pp.202-216). London: Sage.

Fassinger, R., & Morrow, S. L. (2013). Toward best practices in quantitative, qualitative, and mix method research: A Social justice perspective. *Journal for Social Action in Counseling and Psychology, 5*(2), 69-83.

Fechter, A. (2010). Gender, empire, global capitalism: Colonial and corporate expatriate wives." *Journal of Ethnic and Migration Studies* 36 (8): 1279–97.

Finlay, L. (2006). Mapping methodology. In L. Finlay & C. Ballinger (Eds.), *Qualitative research for allied health professionals: Challenging choices.* Chichester, England: John Wiley & Sons.

Fischer, C. T. (2009). Bracketing in qualitative research: Conceptual and practical matters. *Psychotherapy Research, 19*(4-5), 583-590.

Finch, J. (2012). *Married to the job: Wives' incorporation in men's work* (Vol. 20). Routledge.

Flick, U. (2009). *An Introduction to Qualitative Research* (4th ed).

London: Sage.

Frame, M. W., & Shehan, C. L. (1994). Work and well-being in the two-person career: Relocation stress and coping among clergy husbands and wives. *Family relations*, 196-205.

Franke, J., & Nicholson, N. (2002). Who shall we send? Cultural and other influences on the rating of selection criteria for expatriate assignments. *International Journal of Cross Cultural Management*, 2(1), 21-36.

Gadamer, H. G. (1975). *Truth and method* (W. Glen-Dopel, Trans.). London: Sheed and Ward. (Original work published 1960).

Gergen, K. J. (1985). The social constructionist movement in modern psychology. *American Psychologist*, 40(3), 266-275.

Gergen, K. J. (1987). *Toward self as relationship*. In K. Yardley & T. Honess (Eds), *Self and Identity: Psychological Perspectives* (pp.53-63). Chichester: John Wiley.

Giddens, A. (1991). *Modernity and self-Identity: Self and society in the late modern age*. Stanford, California: Stanford University Press.

Giddens, A. (2002). *Runaway world: How globalization is reshaping our lives?* London: Profile Books.

Gilboa-Schechtman, E., Friedman, L., Helpman, L., & Kananov, J. (2013). Self-evaluations of social rank and affiliation in social anxiety: Explicit and implicit measures. *International Journal of Cognitive Therapy*, 6(3), 208–220.

Gilbert P. 1992. *Depression: The Evolution of Powerlessness*. Lawrence Erlbaum Associates: Hove; Guilford: New York.

Gilbert, P. (2000). The relationship of shame, social anxiety and depression: The role of the evaluation of social rank. *Clinical Psychology & Psychotherapy*, 7(3), 174–189.

Gill, H. L., & Haurin, D. R. (1998). Wherever he may go: How wives affect their husband's career decisions. *Social Science Research*, 27(3), 264-279.

Giorgi, A. (2009). *The descriptive phenomenological method in psychology: A modified Husserlian approach.* Pittsburgh, VA: Duquesne University Press.

Glaser, B. G., & Strauss, A. L. (1967). *The discovery of grounded theory: Strategies for qualitative research.* Chicago: Aldine Publishing Company.

Goffman, E. (1959). *The presentation of self in everyday life.* New York: Anchor Books.

Goffman, E. (2001). The presentation of self in everyday life. In A. Branaman, A. Branaman (Eds.) , *Self and society* (pp. 175-182). Malden: Blackwell Publishing.

Greenberg, L. S., Watson, J. C., & PsycBOOKS. (2005;2006;). *Emotion-focused therapy for depression* (1st ed.). Washington, DC: American Psychological Association.

Hall, S. (1996) 'Who Needs Identity?', in S. Hall and P. du Gay (eds) *Questions of Cultural Identity.* London: Sage.

Hall, S., & Du Gay, P. (1996). *Questions of cultural identity.* London: SAGE.

Halling, S., Leifer, M., & Rowe, J.O. (2006). Emergence of the dialogal approach: Forgiving another. In C. T. Fischer (Ed.), *Qualitative Research Methods for Psychology: Introduction through Empirical Studies* (pp. 247-278). New York: Academic Press.

Haslberger, A. (2005), The complexities of expatriate adaptation, *Human Resource Management Review*, 15(2), 160-180.

Haslberger, A., & Brewster, C. (2008). The expatriate family: An international perspective. *Journal of Managerial Psychology, 23*(3), 324-346.

Hardwick, S. (2003). Migration embedded networks and social capital: Towards theorizing North American ethnic geography. *International Journal of Population Geography* 9: 163–179.

Hargie, O. (1997). *The handbook of communication skills.* Hove, England: Psychology Press.

Haring, M., Hewitt, P. L., & Flett, G. L. (2003). Perfectionism, coping, and quality of intimate relationships. *Journal of Marriage & Family*, 65, 143–158.

Harrist, S. (2006). A phenomenological investigation of the experience of ambivalence. *Journal of Phenomenological Psychology, 37(1),* 85-114.

Harvey, M. (1985), The executive family: An overlooked variable in international assignments, *Columbia Journal of World Business*, 20(2), 84-92.

Heidegger, M. (1962). *Being and Time* (J. Macquarrie & E. Robinson, Trans.). New York: Harper & Row. (Original work published 1927).

Hendry A. (1998), "From Parallel to Dual Careers: Diplomatic Spouses in the European Context," in Kurbalija, *Modern Diplomacy* pp. 127-145.

Hendry, J., Watson, CW. (2001). *An anthropology of indirect communication*. London: Routledge; 2001.

Henwood, K. L., & Pidgeon, N. F. (1992). Qualitative research and psychological theorizing. *British Journal of Psychology, 83*, 97-111.

Hochschild, A. R. (1997). Marriage, family and economics: The time bind: When work becomes home and home becomes work. In J. M. Henslin, J. M. Henslin (Eds.) , *Down to earth sociology: Introductory readings (12th ed.)* (pp. 379-389). New York, NY, US: Free Press.

Hochschild, A. R. (2005). On the edge of the time bind: Time and market culture. *Social Research, 72*(2), 339-354.

Hockings, B. (2006). Multistakeholder diplomacy: Forms, functions and frustrations. In J. Kurbaljia & E. Katrandjiev (Eds.), *Multistakeholder diplomacy: Challenges and opportunities.* Geneva: Diplo Foundation.

Holmes, T. H., & Rahe, R. H. (1967). The social re-adjustment rating scale. *Journal of Psychoso- matic Research, 11*, 213-218.

Howard, J.A. (2000). Social psychology of identities. *Annual Review of Sociology*, 26, 367-393.

Hulbert, K. D., & Schuster, D. T. (1993). *Women's lives through time: Educated American women of the twentieth century.* San

Francisco, CA: Jossey-Bass.

Husserl, E. (1927). "Phenomenology". Edmund Husserl's article for the Encyclopaedia Britannica (R.E. Palmer, Trans.). Retrieved 21 January 2017 from: http://www.hfu.edu.tw/~huangkm/phenom/husserl-britanica.htm#_ftn1

Hyslop, L. (2012), Expat divorce in Dubai on the rise, *The Telegraph*, May 2, p. 5.

Ismail, M., Ali, A. J., & Shaharudin, M. R. (2015). Repatriate Children's Readjustment to the Home Country and the Impact on Repatriates. *Asian Social Science*, *11*(25), 25.

Jaspal, R. (2011). Caste, social stigma and identity processes. *Psychology & Developing Societies, 23*(1), 27-62.

Jaspal, R., & Cinnirella, M. (2010). Coping with potentially incompatible identities: Accounts of religious, ethnic, and sexual identities from British Pakistani men who Identify as Muslim and gay. *British Journal of Social Psychology, 49*(4), 849-870.

Jenkins, R. (2008). *Social identity.*, 3rd ed. New York, NY, US: Routledge/Taylor &

Francis Group.

Jones, S. R. (1997). Voices of identity and difference: A qualitative exploration of the multiple dimensions of identity development in women college students. *Journal of College Student Development, 38(4),* 376-386.

Kanji, S., & Cahusac, E. (2015). Who am I? mothers' shifting identities, loss and sensemaking after workplace exit. *Human Relations*, 68(9), 1415-1436.

Kasket, E. (2012). The Counseling psychologist researcher. *Counseling Psychology Review, 27* (2), 64-73.

Kelly, J. G. (1970). Antidotes for arrogance: Training for community psychology. *American Psychologist*, *25*(6), 524-531.

Kim, K.S. & Lee, E.Y., (2011). Social media as information source: Undergraduates' use and evaluation behavior. *Proceedings of the American Society for Information Science and Technology*, *48*(1), 1-3.

Kinsley, S. (1977). Women's dependency and federal programs. In J. R. Chapman & M. Gates (Eds.), Women into wives: The legal and economic impact of marriage (pp. 79–91). Beverly Hills: Sage.

Kraimer, M.L. and Wayne, S.J. (2004), "An examination of perceived organizational support as a multidimensional construct in the context of an expatriate assignment", *Journal of Management*, 30(2), 209-237.

Kramer, M., Wayne, S. and Jaworski, R. (2001), Sources of support and expatriate performance: The mediating role of expatriate adjustment, *Personal Psychology*, 54(1), 71-101.

Krahn, G. L. & Putnam, M. (2003). Qualitative Methods in Psychological Research. In M. C. Roberts & S. S. Ilardi (Eds.), *Handbook of Research Methods in Clinical Psychology* (pp.176-195). Oxford: Blackwell.

Kohonen, E. (2008), The impact of international assignments on expatriates' identity and career aspirations: Reflections upon re-entry, *Scandinavian Journal of Management, 24*, 320-329.

Kupka, B. and Cathro, V. (2007), Desperate housewives: Social and professional isolation of German expatriated spouses, *International Journal of Human Resource Management*, Vol. 18 No. 6, pp. 951-968.

Langdridge, D. (2007). *Phenomenological psychology: Theory, research and method.* Harlow, England: Pearson Education.

Langdridge, D., & Hagger-Johnson, G. (2009). *Introduction to research methods and data analysis in psychology.* Harlow, England: Pearson Education.

Larkin, M., Watts, S., & Clifton, E. (2006). Giving voice and making sense in interpretative phenomenological analysis. *Qualitative Research in Psychology, 3*(2), 102-120.

Lauring, J. and Selmer, J. (2010), The supportive expatriate spouse: An ethnographic study of spouse, *International Business Review*, 19(1), 59-69.

Lazarova, M., McNulty, Y. and Semeniuk, M. (2015), "Expatriate family narratives on international mobility: Key characteristics of the successful moveable family", in Suutari, V. and Makela, L. (Eds), Work and Personal Life Interface of *International Career Contexts*, Springer, Heidelberg, pp. 55-76.

Lazarova, M., Westman, M. and Shaffer, M. (2010), Elucidating the positive side of the work family interface on international assignments: A model of expatriate work and family performance, *Academy of Management Review*, 35(1), 93-117.

Lincoln, Y. S., & Guba, E. G. (1985). *Naturalistic inquiry.* Beverly Hills, CA: SAGE

Publications.

Linstead, A. & Thomas, R (2002). What do you want from me: A poststructuralist feminist reading of middle managers' identities [Electronic version]. *Culture and Organization, 8* (1), 1–20.

Lloyd, V., Gatherer, A., & Kalsy, S. (2006). Conducting qualitative interview research with people with expressive language difficulties. *Qualitative Health Research, 16*(10), 1386-1404.

Lockwood, P., & Kunda, Z. (1997). Superstars and me: Predicting the impact of role models on the self. *Journal of Personality and Social Psychology, 73*(1), 91–103.

Logan, R.D. (1987). Historical change in prevailing sense of self. In K. Yardley, and T. Honess (Eds), *Self and Identity: Psychological Perspectives* (pp. 13-26). Chichester: John Wiley.

Lyons, E., & Coyle, A. (2007). *Analysing qualitative data in psychology.* Thousand Oaks, CA: Sage Publications Ltd.

Madill, A., Jordan, A., & Shirley, C. (2000). Objectivity and reliability in qualitative analysis: Realist, contextualist and radical constructionist epistemologies. *British Journal of Psychology, 91*(1), 20.

Madzia, R. (2013). Mead and self-embodiment: Imitation, simulation, and the problem of taking the attitude of the other. *Österreichische Zeitschrift Für Soziologie, 38*(S1), 195-213.

Margolis, J. & Catudal, J. (2001). *The Quarrel between invariance and flux: A Guide for philosphers and other players.* Pennsylvania: Pennsylvania State University Press.

Marshall, J. (1986). Exploring the experiences of women managers: Towards rigour in qualitative methods. In S. Wilkinson (Ed.), *Feminist social psychology: Developing theory and practice* (pp. 193-209). Milton Keynes, England: Open University Press.

Maxwell, J. A. (2012). *A realist approach for qualitative research.* Sage.

Mcbride, C., & Bagby, R. M. (2006). Rumination and interpersonal dependency: Explaining women's vulnerability to depression. *Canadian Psychology/Psychologie Canadienne,* 47(3), 184-194.

McCall, G. J., & Simmons, J. L. (1978). *Identities and interactions: An examination of human associations in everyday life* (Rev. ed.). New York: Free Press.

McCarthy, H. (2014). Women, marriage and work in the British diplomatic service. *Women's History Review, 23*(6), 853-873.

McHugh, K. (2000). Inside, outside, upside down, backward,

forward, round and round: A case for ethnographic studies in migration. *Progress in Human Geography* 24 (1): 71–89.

McNulty, Y. (2012), Being dumped in to sink or swim': An empirical study of organizational support for the trailing spouse. *Human Resource Development International*, 15(4), 417-434.

McNulty, Y. (2015). Till stress do us part: The causes and consequences of expatriate divorce. *Journal of Global Mobility*, 3(2), 106-136.

Mead, G. H., 1863-1931, & Morris, C. W. (1934). *Mind, self and society: From the standpoint of a social behaviorist* (1st reprint ed.). London;Chicago;: University of Chicago Press.

Meier, L. 2016. Dwelling in different localities: Identity performances of a white transnational professional elite in the city of London and the central business district of Singapore. *Cultural Studies* 30 (3): 483–505.

Meier, A., Reinecke, L., & Meltzer, C. E. (2016). "Facebocrastination"? Predictors of using Facebook for procrastination and its effects on students' well-being. *Computers in Human Behavior*, *64*, 65–76.

Miller, G. A. (1969). Psychology as a means of promoting human welfare. *American Psychologist*, *24*(12), 1063-1075.

Mohr, A. and Klein, S. (2004), Exploring the adjustment of American expatriate spouses in Germany. *International Journal of Human Resource Management*, 15(7), 1189-1206.

Moore, T. & Rae, J. (2009). Outsiders': How some Counseling psychologists construct themselves. *Counseling Psychology Quarterly, 22(4),* 381-392.

Nadkarni, A., & Hofmann, S. G. (2012). Why do people use Facebook? *Personality and Individual Differences, 52,* 243–249.

Nicholson, N. (1984). A theory of work role transitions. *Administrative Science Quarterly, 29*(2), 172-191.

Niekrenz, Y., Witte, M. D., & Albrecht, L. (2016). Transnational lives. transnational bodies? an introduction. *Transnational Social Review*, 6(1-2), 93-95.

Nolen-Hoeksema, S., & Davis, C. G. (1999). "Thanks for sharing that": Ruminators and their social support networks. *Journal of*

Personality and Social Psychology, 77, 801-814.

Nye, J. S. (1991). *Bound to lead: The changing nature of american power* ([New]. ed.). New York: Basic Books.

Ortiz, S. M. (1997). Traveling with the ball club: A code of conduct for wives only. *Symbolic Interaction, 20*(3), 225-249.

Pahl, J. M., & Pahl, R. E. (1971). *Managers and their wives: A study of career and family relationships in the middle class.* Lane, Allen.

Palmer, A., & Parish, J. (2008). Social justice and Counseling psychology: Situating the role of graduate student research, education, and training. *Canadian Journal of Counseling, 42*(4), 278–292.

Pan, Z., Lu, Y., Wang, B. and Chau, P.Y., (2017). Who do you think you are? Common and differential effects of social self-identity on social media usage. *Journal of Management Information Systems, 34* (1), pp.71-101.

Papanek, H. (1973). Men, women, and work: Reflections on the two-person career. *American Journal of Sociology*, 78(4), 852-872.

Patton, MQ. (2001). *Qualitative Evaluation and Research Methods (2nd Edition).* Thousand oaks, CA: Sage Publications.

Pearlin, L. and Johnson, J. (1977), "Marital status, life-stains and depression", *American Sociological Review*, 42(5), 704-715.

Permits Foundation (2018), International Survey of Expatriate Spouses and Partners: Employment, Work Permits and International Mobility, *Permits Foundation,* The Hague.

Pietkiewicz, I., & Smith, J. A. (2014). A practical guide to using interpretative phenomenological analysis in qualitative research psychology. *Psychological Journal, 20*(1), 7-14.

Ponterotto, J. G. (2005). Qualitative research in counseling psychology: A primer on research paradigms and philosophy of science. *Journal Of Counseling Psychology, 52*(2), 126-136.

Potter, J. & Wetherell, M. (1987). *Discourse and social psychology: Beyond attitudes and behaviour.* London: Sage.

Rafalin, D. (2010). Counseling psychology and research: Revisiting the relationship in the light of our 'mission'. In M. Milton (Ed.), *Therapy and Beyond: Counseling psychology contributions to therapeutic and social issues* (p41 – 55). Oxford, UK: Wiley-Blackwell.

Ravasi, C., Salamin, X., & Davoine, E. (2013). *The challenge of dual career expatriate management in a specific host national environment: An exploratory study of expatriate and spouse adjustment in Switzerland based MNCs.* Université de Fribourg.

Reid, K., Flowers, P., & Larkin, M. (2005). Exploring lived experience. *The Psychologist,* 18(1), 20-23.

Reid, P. T., & Kelly, E. (1994). Research on women of color: From ignorance to awareness. *Psychology of Women Quarterly,* 18, 477–486.

Reid, P. T., Cole, E., & Kern, M. L. (2011). Wives of college and university presidents: Identity, privacy, and relationships. *Psychology of Women Quarterly, 35*(4), 547-557.

Rifkind, L. J. (2000). Breaking out of the circle: An analysis of the gendered communication behaviors of Hillary Clinton and Sarah Netanyahu. *The Social Science Journal, 37*, 611–618.

Riordan, S. 2003. *The New Diplomacy.* Cambridge: Polity Press.

Robbins, S. B., & Jolkovski, M. P. (1987). Managing countertransference feelings: An interactional model using awareness of feeling and theoretical framework. *Journal of Counseling Psychology, 34*(3), 276-282.

Rosenbusch, K. and Cseh, M. (2012), The cross-cultural adjustment process of expatriate families in a multinational organization: a family system theory perspective. *Human Resource Development International, 15*(1), 61-77.

Salomon, G. (1991). Transcending the qualitative-quantitative debate: The analytic and systemic approaches to educational research. *Educational researcher, 20*(6), 10-18.

Schmidt, L. K. (2016). *Understanding hermeneutics.* Routledge.

Schleiermacher, F. (1998). *Hermeneutics and criticism and other writings* (A. Bowie, Trans.). Cambridge, England: Cambridge University Press. (Original work published 1838).

Seale, C. (1999). Quality in qualitative research. *Qualitative Inquiry, 5*(4), 465 478.

Searle, W. and Ward, C. (1990), The prediction of psychological and sociocultural adjustment during cross-cultural transition. *International Journal of Intercultural Relations,* 14(4), 449-464.

Sedikides, C., & Gregg, A. (2003). *Portraits of the self.* In M. A. Hogg & J. Cooper (Eds.), Sage handbook of social psychology (pp. 110–138). London: Sage.

Shaffer, M. and Harrison, D. (1998), Expatriates' psychological withdrawal from international assignments: Work, non-work, and family influences. *Personnel Psychology*, 51(1), 87-118.

Shaffer, M., Harrison, D., Gilley, K. and Luk, D. (2001). Struggling for balance amid turbulence on international assignments: Work/family conflict, support, and commitment. *Journal of Management*, 27(1), 99-121.

Shilling, C., & Mellor, P. A. (1996). Embodiment, structuration theory and modernity: Mind/body dualism and the repression of sensuality. *Body & Society, 2*(4), 1-15.

Silverman, D. (2013). *Doing qualitative research (Fourth ed.). Los Angeles: SAGE*

Silvey, R. and Lawson, V. (1999). Placing the Migrant. *Annals of the Association of American Geographers* 89(1), 121-132.

Simosi, M., Rousseau, D. M., & Daskalaki, M. (2015). When career paths cease to exist: A qualitative study of career behavior in a crisis economy. *Journal of Vocational Behavior*, 91, 134-146.

Smith, J. A. (1996). Beyond the divide between cognition and discourse: Using interpretative phenomenological analysis in health psychology. *Psychology and Health,* 11 (2), 261-271.

Smith, J.A. (2004). Reflecting on the development of interpretative phenomenological analysis and its contribution to qualitative research in psychology. *Qualitative Research in Psychology, 1,* 39–54.

Smith, M.P. and Favell, A. (eds) (2006) *The Human Face of Global Mobility: International High Skilled Migrants in Europe, North America and the Asia Pacific.* New Bruswick, NJ: Transaction Press.

Smith, J. A., Flowers, P. & Larkin, M. (2009). *Interpretative Phenomenological Analysis: Theory, Method and Research.* London, UK: Sage.

Smith, J.A, Flowers, P. & Osborn, M. (1997). Interpretative phenomenological analysis and the psychology of health and illness. In L. Yardley (Ed.), *Material Discourses of Health and Illness* (pp. 68-91). London: Routledge.

Smith, J. A., & Osborn, M. (2003). Interpretative phenomenological analysis. In J.

Smith (Ed.), *Qualitative psychology. A practical guide to research methods* (pp. 53-80). London: SAGE Publications.

Smith J.A., & Osborn, M. (2008) Interpretative phenomenological analysis. In: JA Smith, ed. Qualitative psychology: a practical guide to research methods. London: Sage, 53-80.

Spiegelberg, E. (Ed.). (2012). *The phenomenological movement: A historical introduction* (Vol. 5). Springer Science & Business Media.

Spinelli, E. (2005). *The Interpreted World: An Introduction to Phenomenological Psychology.* London, UK: Sage.

Stets, J. E. & Burke, P. J. (2000). Identity theory and social identity theory [Electronic version]. *Social Psychology Quarterly, 63* (3), 224-237.

Strazdins, L., & Broom, D. H. (2004). Acts of love (and work) gender imbalance in emotional work and women's psychological distress. *Journal of Family Issues, 25*(3), 356-378.

Stroud, J. G. (2015). *Cultural influences in research and therapeutic practice: A Counseling psychology perspective* (Doctoral dissertation, City University London).

Stryker, S. and Vryan, K. (2006), *"The symbolic interactionist frame"*, in Delamater, J. (Ed.), Handbook of Social Psychology, Springer, New York, NY, pp. 3-28.

Sweatman, S. (1999). Marital satisfaction, cross-cultural adjustment stress, and the psychological sequelae. *Journal of Psychology and Theology*, 27(2), 154-162.

Tajfel , H. (ed.) (1978 *). Differentiation between social groups* . London: Academic Press.

Tajfel, H., & Turner, J. C. (1986). *The social identity theory of intergroup conflict.* In S. Worchel & W. G. Austin (Eds.), *Psychology of Inter-Group Relations* (pp. 7-24). Chicago: Nelson-Hall.

Takeuchi, R., Yun, S. and Tesluk, P. (2002). An examination of crossover and spillover effects of spousal and expatriate cross cultural adjustment on expatriate outcomes. *Journal of Applied Psychology*, 87(4), 655-666.

Tharenou, P., & Caulfield, N. (2010). "Will I stay or will I go?

Explaining repatriation by self-initiated expatriates". *The Academy of Management Journal, 53*(5), 1009-1028.

Thomas, D. R. (2006). A general inductive approach for analyzing qualitative evaluation data. *American Journal Of Evaluation, 27*(2), 237-246.

Timotijevic, L., & Breakwell, G.M. (2000). Migration and threat to identity. *Journal of Community and Applied Social Psychology*, 10, 355-372.

Todd, V. F. (1995). Who needs curtains anyway? The impact of corporate relocation on the self-concept of trailing wives. *Dissertation Abstracts International, 55*, 4015.

Tosun, L. P. (2012). Motives for Facebook use and expressing the "true self" on the Internet. *Comput- ers in Human Behavior, 28*, 1510–1517.

Tung, R. L. (1998). American expatriates abroad: From neophytes to cosmopolitans. *Journal of World Business, 33*(2), 125-144.

Urry, J. (2000). *Sociology beyond societies: Mobilities for the twenty-first century*. London, UK: Routledge.

Valor-Segura, I., Expósito, F., Moya, M., & Kluwer, E. (2014). Don't leave me: The effect of dependency and emotions in relationship conflict: Dependency, emotions, and conflict. *Journal of Applied Social Psychology*, 44(9), 579-587.

van Bochove, M. and Engbersen, G. (2015), Beyond cosmopolitanism and expat bubbles: challenging dominant representations of knowledge workers and trailing spouses. *Population, Place and Space, 21*. 295-309.

van der Zee, K.I., Ali, A.J. and Salomé, E. (2005), Role interference and subjective well-being among expatriate families. *European Journal of Work and Organizational Psychology*, 14(1), 239-62.

Vignoles, V. L., Regalia, C., Manzi, C., Golledge, J., & Scabini, E. (2006). Beyond self-esteem: Influence of multiple motives on identity construction. *Journal Of Personality And Social Psychology*, 90(2), 308-333.

Vignoles, V. L., Schwartz, S. J., & Luyckx, K. (2011). *Introduction: Toward an integrative view of identity*. In V. L. Vignoles, S. J. Schwartz & K. Luyckx (Eds.), Handbook of identity theory and research (pp. 1-27). New York: Springer.

Vitak, J., & Ellison, N. B. (2013). "There's a network out there you might as well tap": Exploring the benefits of and barriers to exchanging informational and support-based resources on Facebook. *New Media & Society, 15*(2), 243–259

Vogel, E. A., Rose, J. P., Roberts, L. R., & Eckles, K. (2014). Social comparison, social media, and self-esteem. *Psychology of Popular Media Culture, 3*(4), 206–222.

Ward, C. and Kennedy, A. (1993). Psychological and sociocultural adjustment during cross-cultural transitions: A comparison of secondary students overseas and at home. *International Journal of Psychology,* 28(2), 129-147.

Ward, C., Okura, Y., Kennedy, A. and Kojima, T. (1998), The U-curve on trial: A longitudinal study of psychological and sociocultural adjustment during cross-cultural transition. *International Journal of Intercultural Relations.* 22(3). 277-291.

Wilkinson, A. and Singh, G. (2010). Managing stress in the expatriate family: A case study of the state department of the United States of America. *Public Personnel Management.* 39(2). 169-181.

Wille-Romer, G. (1992). *Zur Situation der Ehefrauen, BMaA-Studie 1991/92, Teil B.*

Willig, C. (2008). *Introducing qualitative research in psychology: Adventures in theory and method* (2nd ed.). Maidenhead, England: McGraw-Hill.

Willig, C. (2012). Perspectives on the Epistemological Bases for Qualitative Research. In H. Cooper (Ed.), *The Handbook of Research Methods in Psychology:* Vol.1. Foundations, Planning, Measures and Psychometrics (pp.1-17). Washington DC: American Psychological Association.

Willig, C. (2013). *Introducing qualitative research in psychology.* McGraw-Hill Education (UK).

Willig, C., & Stainton-Rogers, W. (2008). *The SAGE handbook of qualitative research in psychology.* London: SAGE Publications.

Wolniewicz, C. A., Tiamiyu, M. F., Weeks, J. W., & Elhai, J. D. (2017). Problematic smartphone use and relations with negative affect, fear of missing out, and fear of negative and positive evaluation. *Psychiatry Research.*

Woods, H. C., & Scott, H. (2016). pass:[#]Sleepyteens: Social media use in adolescence is associated with poor sleep quality, anxiety, depression and low self-esteem. *Journal of Adolescence, 51,* 41–49.

Yardley, L. (2008). Demonstrating validity in qualitative research. In J. A. Smith

(Ed.), *Qualitative psychology: A practical guide to research methods* (pp. 235 251). London: SAGE Publications.

Yellig, A. (2011). The experiences of married international graduate students and their accompanying non-student spouses in the u.s. culture: A qualitative study. *Dissertation Abstracts International, 71,* 5167.

Zuo, J., & Shengming, T. (2000). Breadwinner status and gender ideologies of men and women regarding family roles. *Sociological Perspectives,* 43, 29–43.